ALL ABOUT
Paperweights

ALL ABOUT
Paperweights

LAWRENCE H. SELMAN

PAPERWEIGHT PRESS · SANTA CRUZ, CALIFORNIA

On the cover:

1. Victor Trabucco citron blossom
2. Modern Saint Louis encased overlay
3. Modern Baccarat Gridel monkey
4. Ken Rosenfeld Virginia bluebells
5. Parabelle Glass close concentric millefiori
6. Antique Baccarat close packed millefiori
7. Antique Baccarat miniature rose
8. Antique Saint Louis pompon on latticinio
9. Antique Saint Louis fruit on latticinio
10. Parabelle Glass blossom on lace
11. Antique Saint Louis looped garland
12. Perthshire miniature swirl
13. Randall Grubb single grape cluster
14. Antique Saint Louis concentric millefiori
15. John Deacons clematis
16. Clichy garland with central rose
17. Perthshire miniature crown
18. Modern Saint Louis magnum bouquet
19. Rick Ayotte Illusion fall bouquet
20. Debbie Tarsitano circular plaque
21. Rick Ayotte Eastern bluebird
22. Paul Stankard lady's-slipper orchids
23. Paul Stankard botanical block

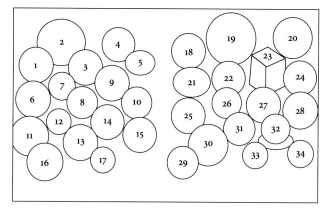

24. Bob Banford gingham-cut overlay bouquet
25. Lundberg Studios sterling rose
26. Antique Saint Louis bouquet with torsade
27. Antique Saint Louis fuchsia on latticinio
28. Antique Baccarat pansy
29. Antique Saint Louis encased overlay bouquet
30. Chris Buzzini braided stem bouquet
31. Charles Kaziun silhouette
32. New England Glass Company blown apple
33. Charles Kaziun concentric millefiori with silhouettes
34. Modern Saint Louis commemorative crown

Frontispiece:

Clichy miniature close concentric millefiori with fifteen Clichy roses

First published 1992
Printed in Japan by Dai Nippon Printing Company

Set in Adobe Minion using Aldus PageMaker

Library of Congress Cataloging-in-Publication Data:

Selman, Lawrence.
    All about paperweights / Lawrence H. Selman.
      p. cm.
    Includes bibliography.
    ISBN 0-933756-17-8 : $24.95
    1. Paperweights—History. I. Title.
  NK5440.P3S42   1992
  748.8'4—dc20

Table of Contents

Contemporary Paperweights (continued)

Foreword

I am very fortunate to have been connected with the field of paperweights for more than twenty years. In that time I have seen it transformed from a position of relative obscurity into an area of great interest and popularity. Today, many talented young artists are entering the field, making weights that equal the antiques in beauty and design. Collectors worldwide continue to seek both hard-to-find antique pieces and fine contemporary works. For the seasoned connoisseur and novice collector alike, this is a very exciting time—a paperweight renaissance.

As Paperweight Press we have published many books on the subject, starting with *Paperweights for Collectors* in 1975 and followed by histories of specific artists and factories, books about identification, and exhibition catalogues. *The Art of the Paperweight*, published in 1988, is recognized the world over as the most comprehensive and authoritative book about paperweights. As new areas of interest opened up, we have provided books to fill the demand for information. The main purpose of *All About Paperweights* is to offer the general public an attractive, inexpensive and accessible book about paperweights. People who have never before seen these small beautiful works of art can learn about their rich history, how they are made and who makes them.

Early collectors did not have the advantage of reference books or catalogues to aid them in acquiring weights. They relied on intuition and personal taste to choose pieces for their collections. Happily, this is no longer true. Let this book serve as your introduction and guide to a fascinating world.

Collecting Paperweights

Introduction

> *"Why do men and women collect? As well ask why they fall in love; the reasons are as irrational, the motives as mixed, the original impulse as often discolored or betrayed. The collector's instinct, if animals and children are any guide, has two roots; the desire to pick up anything bright and shining and the desire to complete a series. . . . The finest collectors look at their possessions with the feelings of an artist and relive, to some extent, the sensuous and imaginative experiences which lie behind each work."*
> (Frank Manheim, *A Garland of Weights*)

Paperweight collecting often begins with a fascination for these unusual pieces; the awareness of an obscure and compelling art form. Then comes the desire to know more about them: who made them, how are they made, where did they come from, who else collects them, their inherent worth and value. In the following excerpt from *The Encyclopedia of Glass Paperweights,* Paul Hollister describes the initial questioning stage of collecting paperweights: "Precisely what is it, one asks, that is inside this paperweight? And continues to ask even when one knows it is simply colored glass. We are gazing into a mystery whose true dimensions and physical composition our senses are unable to pinpoint, a mystery sealed away in perpetuity. You may look at it but you cannot touch it."

After research comes the realization that paperweights have a rich and glorious history. Exactly why the great glasshouses of France (Baccarat, Saint Louis and Clichy) began making paperweights in the mid-1800s remains a mystery. Some scholars believe that the perfection of the millefiori paperweight process was being

◀ *A diverse collection of paperweights and related objects* developed concurrently in Venice, France, and Bohemia during early 1840s. There is no dispute, however, about which country quickly assumed the lead in paperweight production. By 1845 France was the undeniable paperweight center of the world. In a remarkably short period of time, the French glass factories had perfected the millefiori technique and introduced and developed the lampwork style. English glass factories were quick to imitate the techniques of the French makers, as were those in the United States, where paperweight production began and ended significantly later than in France. Just as mysterious as their initial appearance and fantastic popularity was their sudden inexplicable decline. After about 1860 the art of paperweight making all but disappeared for eighty years.

The paperweights made in France during the classic period remain as inspiration to modern glass artists, who today consider the making of these art pieces the basis of a life's work. Fine contemporary paperweights are now considered to be as well-crafted and as collectible as the antiques.

Collecting glass paperweights often starts as a personal thrill and grows to become a lifelong passion. The weights themselves reflect the nature and sensibilities of the artist; a collection reflects the personal taste, style, and focus of the collector. Collections of excellence can be based on many factors: style, theme, color, technique, or maker. Particular designs, such as single flowers, floral bouquets, or fruit clusters give ample opportunity for specialized theme collections. An exquisite collection can also be formed by selecting a group of weights from one artist or one studio.

The well-known French writer Colette decorated her apartment in the Palais Royale with paperweights, many of which she found in Paris flea markets. King Farouk, Queen Mary, Eva Perón, Truman Capote, Robert Guggenheim, and scores of other famous and infamous personalities have been serious collectors.

The earliest major English paperweight collector was Mrs. Applewhaite-Abbott, who built a collection of several hundred weights between 1900 and 1938. Three hundred of these were sold at auction for $90,000 by Sotheby's in 1952. According to her records, she paid as little as two shillings and not more than £26 for any one of these weights.

Mrs. Evangeline Bergstrom, wife of a Wisconsin paper manufacturer, began her huge collection shortly after the turn of the century. She wrote *Old Glass Paperweights* in 1940, the first serious American effort to describe the history and manufacture of paperweights. Her collection is now housed at the Bergstrom-Mahler Museum in Neenah, Wisconsin.

As one example of the rise in value of a single paperweight, consider the fascinating history of the Pantin silkworm weight. It was first bought by Mrs. Applewhaite-Abbott in the late 1920s for £26 ($125). When her collection was sold at auction by Sotheby's in 1953, this one weight sold for £1200. It was purchased at auction for King Farouk by a dealer. However, the day of the auction King Farouk abdicated his throne and the dealer was left with the piece. It was later sold again, and eventually purchased by Paul Jokelson. When the Jokelson collection was sold at Sotheby's in 1983, this weight was bought by Arthur Rubloff for the record-breaking price of $143,000. Rubloff gave his entire collection including the prized Pantin weight to the Chicago Art Institute, where it is now on permanent display.

A similar collector's story revolves around another of Paul Jokelson's prized paperweights, the "Bird in the Nest." In 1925, while browsing through the antique shops on the rue des Saint Péres in Paris, a youthful Jokelson spied what he later discovered was a paperweight with a bird in a nest. Although the dealer knew nothing of its history, Jokelson liked it and purchased it for approximately $25. Intrigued, he went on the search for other paperweights in order to learn more about them. Jokelson was soon on his way to collecting antique French paperweights and then sulphides. In 1953, by which time he was an importer and avid collector, he wanted a sulphide of General Eisenhower. He approached the glass factories of Baccarat and

Collection based on floral motifs

Saint Louis with the idea of reviving the classic art. This was a difficult and challenging proposition, since paperweights had not been produced in significant numbers for more than eighty years. Artists and craftsmen spent nearly twenty years in research and experimentation rediscovering the techniques used in making sulphide, millefiori, and lampwork paperweights. Once they succeeded, interest in contemporary paperweights blossomed. As for the "Bird in the Nest," in 1990 it realized the record-breaking price of $182,600 at an L. H. Selman Ltd. auction.

Developing a Collection

Many people start with Colette's method of selecting weights for a collection. She chose only what enchanted her, and did not concentrate or fret over small imperfections in the pieces. In her Paris flat her collection literally surrounded her and the sight of these "small frozen gardens" never ceased to bring her great joy. Of her mother's collecting Colette de Jouvenel said, "What would all the vigilant collectors think . . . of the off-hand manner with

Weights with aquatic themes

which my mother gleaned her weights haphazardly during her walks, without being obsessive about it, but with the sign of joy given by the lucky finds at first sight absurd or modest?"

Most collectors, however, soon begin to develop a strategy. There are many different approaches to collecting paperweights. The reason for collecting makes a vast difference in the collection that develops. If one collects strictly for fun, Colette's method is perfect. Pick what pleases the eye and do not be concerned with long-term calculations. On the other hand, if one is collecting strictly for investment potential, strategy and knowledge of the field must be developed quickly. Happily, most collectors are somewhere in between, with a strong appreciation of the beauty and uniqueness of paperweights, along with an intelligent awareness of their value.

Collections can be built exclusively on antique pieces; contemporary annual editions from Baccarat, Saint Louis, or Perthshire; or fine weights by American studio artists. No matter what approach is taken, the key to developing a good collection is knowledge and attention to quality. Collecting and investing in paperweights is a challenge. This challenge is met with expert advice and prudent buying. As in all fields of collecting, the need to rely on outside expertise decreases as knowledge grows.

What to Look for in a Paperweight

The factors which considerably influence the value of a piece are design, workmanship, condition and rarity.

Like beauty, design is in the eye of the beholder. Good color and pleasing arrangement of canes, flowers, or other motifs are extremely important. Acquiring a first-rate paperweight collection, therefore, rests heavily on the collector's ability to evaluate good design.

Fortunately, workmanship can be judged objectively. Poor or faulty workmanship shows up in a weight as an imperfection. Although few weights are flawless, major imperfections mar the value of a piece. All true paperweight artists exercise a high degree of quality control so that obviously defective pieces rarely become available. Seconds are systematically destroyed. The collector whose primary consideration is investment should attempt to acquire only first-quality examples.

Here is a checklist of common imperfections found in paper-weight motifs:
- Design not well centered
- Design too close to top or sides of dome
- Millefiori canes broken
- Millefiori canes unevenly spaced
- Millefiori canes missing or overcrowded in garland motifs
- Concentric circles of millefiori canes distorted
- Bubbles
- Leaves, stems, or flower petals separated
- Leaves, stems, or flower petals misshapen
- Spiral torsade or air rings incomplete
- Color ground or latticinio cushion broken

In addition, the glass surrounding the subject should be carefully scrutinized. Imperfections in any part of the glass have a direct influence on the relative value of a paperweight.

The overall condition of a paperweight must be considered when contemplating its purchase. Scratches, chips, and bruises may appear on the surface. If enough glass is present in the dome, the weight may be saved by grinding and polishing, a process that involves removing an even layer of glass from the entire weight. Poor grinding and polishing can easily ruin the original shape and optics of the weight by creating an uneven surface that distorts the design.

Proper grinding and polishing of a paperweight with sufficient surrounding glass does not devalue it; however, it is critical that such work be done by a professional. The value of some weights has been lowered to as little as ten percent of the original value by poor polishing jobs. Consult with an experienced dealer or collector for the name of a professional conservator.

Generally, the more complicated a weight's production, the more desirable it is thought to be. However, an unusual color, date, or flower in a more common design may affect its value and availability. For instance, the presence of a certain identifiable cane (i.e., silhouette cane or Clichy rose) is a plus. Signatures and/or dates are an uncommon bonus in antique weights; in fine modern weights their inclusion is imperative.

One of the questions most commonly asked by beginning collectors is "How can you tell if a paperweight is an antique?" Unfortunately, it is difficult to answer this question simply and without qualification. Train your eye by examining as many weights as possible, studying photographs, reading, and consulting with knowledgeable collectors and dealers whenever possible. As you become familiar with the subtleties and details that make up fine quality paperweights you will be able to determine the general age of a piece.

A variety of fruit designs

Purchasing Paperweights

Even today, choice paperweights can still be found at flea markets and dusty antique shops for incredibly low prices. But this is extremely rare. Serious collectors find most of their pieces through paperweight dealers, private sales, and in auction houses.

The rarest and finest antique and modern weights command top prices. But a quality collection can be formed at a reasonable cost. Among antique weights, scrambled and simple millefiori are generally the least expensive. Some modern limited editions are also moderately priced.

Wise paperweight purchases can offer collectors an excellent investment opportunity. Although the market for many other types of glass, especially American art glass and French cameo glass, has experienced broad fluctuations based on fads and fashion, the antique and contemporary paperweight market has shown a steady rise in value. It is important to consult with experts, research pieces carefully, and deal with reputable dealers.

Keep in mind that the most important aspect of paperweight collecting is to enjoy yourself and your collection. The obstacles and difficulties are precisely what make the activity compelling.

Antique Paperweights

Baccarat close packed millefiori

FRENCH FACTORIES

"The beauty and extraordinary richness of design of the first French paperweights are overwhelming. Their exquisite loveliness and perfection of execution display the workmanship of surpassingly skilled artists in glass about whom nothing, or almost nothing, is known. While many phases of the development of paperweights have been explored and described, the artistic origins are, and must remain, a mystery as baffling as is the inspiration and genesis of most works of art."
(Frank J. Manheim, *A Garland of Weights*)

In a brief but glorious fifteen-year period—1845 to 1860—the great French factories of Baccarat, Saint Louis and Clichy created some of the most remarkable paperweights ever produced. This period of time is called the classic period. The paperweights created in France during this era were greatly admired and imitated throughout the rest of Europe and America, where glass factories continued designing paperweights in the classic style long after the French had ceased production.

Clichy concentric millefiori piedouche

It is not known exactly when the French factories first began producing paperweights, but by the mid-1840s millefiori weights were being produced in large quantities. A short while later the lampwork style was introduced and then developed to include a wide range of flowers, fruits and creatures.

An amazing spectrum of colors and designs are found in these pieces. Many have survived intact to the present day with a beauty that continues to awe, inspire and delight contemporary artists and collectors.

Saint Louis crown

◀ *Baccarat carpet ground with Gridel silhouettes, Baccarat butterfly, Baccarat upright bouquet with torsade, Saint Louis cherries, Baccarat wallflower with cane bud*

Baccarat

Close packed millefiori mushroom

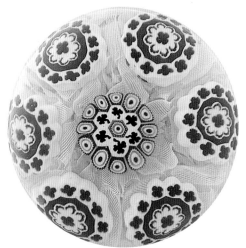

*Spaced concentric millefiori on lace
with shamrock canes*

"Because of its predominance, which was due both to the quality of its crystal and its high output, it did not seek to solicit customers by manufacturing fantasy objects and novelties such as paperweights . . . As soon as a new product was successful, however, Baccarat would jump in and place products of superior quality on the market. Its millefiori testify to a perfection of technique which would remain unsurpassed." (Roger Imbert and Yolande Amic, *Les Presse-Papiers Français de Cristal*)

The company that is today called Compagnie des Cristalleries de Baccarat was founded in 1764, under the name Verrerie de Sainte Anne, by Monseigneur de Montmorency-Laval, Bishop of Metz. Located in the Alsace-Lorraine region of France, within fifty miles of the future site of Cristalleries de Saint Louis, the Verrerie

Spaced concentric millefiori with central arrow canes

18

Scattered millefiori and silhouette canes on upset muslin

Bouquet

Scrambled or macédoine

de Sainte Anne specialized in plate glass, mirrors and a wide range of utilitarian glassware. The location was strategically chosen, for the bishop believed that the best way to utilize his vast forest and help the many unemployed woodcutters in the region was to establish a wood-burning glassworks. Housing for the workers was constructed around the factory, and gradually a small community developed. One report states that immediately prior to the French Revolution in 1789, the factory employed over four hundred workers.

As happened in many eighteenth-century factories, conditions at Verrerie de Sainte Anne deteriorated dramatically from 1790 until the fall of Napoléon in 1815. In 1811 the company shut down two furnaces and kept only seventy of its four hundred workers.

Double overlay

Pompon

Butterfly with garland of canes

In 1816, the factory was sold to M. Aimé-Gabriel d'Artigues, who had worked as director of the Saint Louis factory. Under his direction, the glassworks improved rapidly, becoming France's foremost glassworks by 1822. Baccarat produced the most beautiful crystal in the world; the heaviest (because of its 32% lead content), the most refractive, and the most luminous. In 1823 d'Artigues sold the company and it was renamed Compagnie des Cristalleries de Baccarat.

In 1846, under the management of Emile Godard, the craftsmen at Baccarat perfected the production of millefiori paperweights. By 1848 exquisite lampwork flowers, bouquets, butterflies and other motifs were also being produced. Paperweight manufacture at Baccarat was a small but significant part of the company's production for almost twenty years.

Baccarat excelled in the making of silhouette canes, which were frequently used in carpet grounds, trefoils, mushrooms, overlays and close packed weights. Eighteen of the best-known Baccarat silhouettes, called the Gridel series, were based on the animal cutout designs created in 1847 by Joseph Emile Gridel, the nine-year-old nephew of Jean-Baptiste Toussaint, Baccarat's manager at that time.

Detail of Gridel silhouette canes

Less than a quarter of the antique paperweights made by Baccarat contain date or signature canes. When a signature cane is present it is always accompanied by a date cane; some date canes appear alone. Date canes are comprised of four distinct colored rods fused together, with a single numeral in each rod.

Close concentric millefiori piedouche

Pansy and bud

Double clematis and bud

Clematis buds

Saint Louis

"Mr. Launay of the retail firm of Launay-Hautin and Company correctly stated, 'Paperweights seem to sell well . . .' These encouraging remarks stimulated Saint Louis to continue to produce these artful objects. Because France was going through a period of political agitation, expensive luxuries such as table sets, chandeliers and crystal vases remained unsold. Bad crops and the Revolution of 1848 greatly affected the financial climate of that time. And so, Launay insisted on the making of weights, which were moderately priced and thus easy to sell."
(Gérard Ingold, *The Art of the Paperweight—Saint Louis*)

Cristalleries de Saint Louis was established in 1767, three years after the Cristalleries de Baccarat. Originally named Verrerie Royale de Saint Louis for King Saint Louis of France, the factory was established in the Munzthal forest in the Lorraine region of France. It was an excellent location because of the abundance of wood, sand and potash.

Handcoolers

Pompon

Nosegay with garland of canes

Fuchsia on latticinio

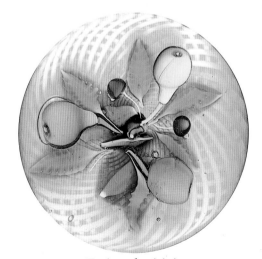

Fruit on latticinio

In the early eighteenth century, France was trailing other European countries in the production of fine glass. In 1760 the Académie Royale des Sciences offered a prize to the factory that could make the best suggestions for improving glass manufacturing techniques. In 1772 the Académie judged that Saint Louis's lead glass was equal in quality to the highly regarded English flint glass. In 1782, under the direction of the Count de Beaufort, Saint Louis was the first glass factory in France to perfect the manufacture of crystal. The industry was deemed important enough that in 1785, the French State Council decreed that a two-year notice must be given in order to resign from the Saint Louis staff, and that permission must be obtained for traveling more than one league from the factory. The transmittal of technological information concerning glass production was a crime punishable by death.

In 1829 the company adopted a new name: Compagnie des Cristalleries de Saint Louis. Two years later, Saint Louis and Baccarat decided to sell their glassware through a retail operation and entered into a joint agreement with the firm of Launay, Hautin et Cie. in Paris.

Scrambled millefiori

Because of its ranking just behind Baccarat, Saint Louis tried to attract customers by developing new lines of articles. Thus it is not surprising that it was the first French factory to show an interest in the production of paperweights. One of its first millefiori weights was dated 1845, and by 1848 Saint Louis was producing a wide range of lampwork pieces as well.

Saint Louis exhibited in many of the Paris exhibitions, but like Baccarat decided not to attend the 1851 Crystal Palace exhibition in London, where Clichy was awarded top honors. The last recorded exhibit of Saint Louis weights was at the Paris Exposition in 1867. Interest in the objects was on the decline and a rich and creative era of paperweight making at Saint Louis was drawing to a close.

Few antique Saint Louis weights are signed or dated. When present, Saint Louis date canes are constructed with the numerals appearing in separate rods fused together with the "SL" cane appearing above the date. The numerals of date canes are done in single colors; either red, blue or black. Date canes are always accompanied by a signature cane; however, there are instances of signature canes appearing alone.

Crown

Jasper panel weight

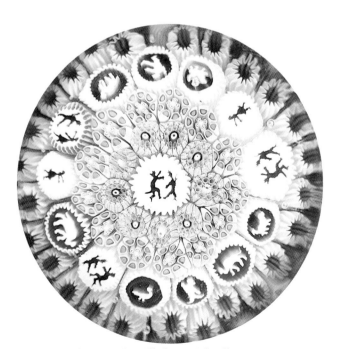

Concentric millefiori with silhouettes

Vase with concentric millefiori base and blue torsade rim

Clichy

Close concentric millefiori

"The collection of Mr. Maez of Clichy, near Paris, is a very extensive and beautiful one. Besides being a manufacturer of glass, he is also well acquainted with the chemical department of his art, as is evinced by the beauty and novelty of some of his productions, for which he has received two medals from his own country and from England at the London Exhibition. The latter was given for lenses and glass for optical instruments; a Council medal for novelty of chemical application, and a prize medal for a prism of zinc glass. . . . Not only is the ornamentation and coloring of Mr. Maez's collection of great merit, but in the design and form of the vessels there is great taste. . . . The paperweights already alluded to, are here in innumerable variety." (Horace Greeley, after seeing the New York Crystal Palace Exhibition at Fifth Avenue and 42nd Street. Quoted by Paul Hollister in *The Encyclopedia of Glass Paperweights*)

Very little recorded information has been found on the third of the three great French factories—Clichy-la-Garenne. Founded by Messrs. Rouyer and Maës, even the founding date and original location are uncertain. Two possibilities are 1837 at Billancourt, or 1838 at Sèvres. It is known that shortly after the business was formed, the operation was moved to Clichy, which is now a suburb of Paris.

Spaced concentric with florets, edelweiss canes, and a central Clichy rose

Swirl with large complex cane center

Spaced concentric millefiori, patterned millefiori, looped garlands on opaque ground, quatrefoil garland, interlaced quatrefoil garlands, "C" scrolls

At first the factory produced inexpensive glass for export, but by the 1840s both Saint Louis and Baccarat were concerned about the company's rapid growth and the improving quality of its glassware. As early as 1844, Clichy exhibited with Baccarat and Saint Louis in Paris, where the young company's exquisite colored and overlay crystal was highly praised.

It is thought that Clichy may have started producing paper-weights as part of a stratagem to entice customers away from the more established glass factories. In a letter to Saint Louis, a Paris retail firm wrote:

> "The selling of weights has now gone mostly to Clichy which cannot fulfill all the orders received. This article [paper-weights] has given a great importance to this factory by the contracts that were established through it with buyers who were not in the habit of applying there."

27

Garland on dark blue

Over the next decade Clichy continued to enjoy a period of growth and success, and in 1851, as the only French factory to show at the Crystal Palace in London, received international acclaim. It has been suggested that Clichy glassworkers were hired by English firms to set up similar production lines because its glass was so highly regarded.

Clichy exhibited at the New York Crystal Palace in 1853, displaying paperweights, perfume bottles, doorknobs and other fine crystal items. The paperweights at this exhibit greatly influenced the production of American weights.

Bouquet

Pink flower with bud

Scrambled or "end-of-day"

After 1870 the quality of Clichy glassware and paperweights declined drastically. A few years later the company was sold to an established glassworks in Sèvres and stopped making paperweights.

Very few Clichy weights are signed. The most frequently used signature cane is a "C" in either serif or sans-serif style. An extremely rare signature is a cane which contains the factory name in full. Clichy also used the "C" scroll garland motif as a signature in some weights.

Sulphide

Close concentric millefiori piedouche, two-color swirl, barber pole chequer, close concentric millefiori piedouche

Pear

Strawberries

Pantin

"Paperweights of solid glass, containing glass snakes, lizards, squirrels and flowers; air-bubbles are distributed in the mass, looking like pearl drops . . . Paperweights in millefiori of roses, leaves and fruit, embedded in clear glass . . . A reptile paperweight, containing a lizard of colored glass, which had been cut in several parts before being inclosed in the glass . . . a coiled snake with head erect, of two colored glasses, cut in spots to show both colors, mounted upon a piece of mirror; an interesting piece of workmanship, showing great dexterity in coiling the snake." (Charles Colné, U.S. delegate to the 1878 Universal Exposition in Paris; quoted by Paul Hollister in *The Encyclopedia of Glass Paperweights*)

In 1850 E. S. Monot established a glassworks at La Villette, near Paris, under the name of Monot et Cie. After moving the company and opening a showroom in Paris, the glass factory moved again to Pantin, No. 84, rue de Paris. By 1873, Monot had been joined by his son and by M. F. Stumpf. The title of the firm was changed at that time to Monot, père et fils, et Stumpf.

The Pantin glassworks produced glass tubes and chemical glassware, as well as fine crystal table glasses, tumblers, perfume bottles and chandeliers. Pantin's wares were said to compare with those of Clichy.

None of the weights now attributed to Pantin were signed or dated. French factories during the classic period were reluctant to allow their wares to be pictured in reports or articles for fear of revealing trade secrets to other manufacturers. From Colné's description, however, it was speculated that several weights formerly unidentified or tentatively attributed to other factories were most probably made by Pantin.

ENGLISH FACTORIES

"The removal of the excise duty led to an explosion in the English glass industry and the results of this explosion were on view six years later at the Great Exhibition [Crystal Palace] in London. Millefiori paperweight production, never as extensive in England as in France, attained quality during those years, its finest efforts being on a par with those of Saint Louis. . . . English millefiori paperweight production of the classic period, confined almost entirely to London and Birmingham, derives stylistically from the concentrics of Baccarat, Saint Louis and Clichy."
(Paul Hollister, *The Encyclopedia of Glass Paperweights*)

During the first part of the eighteenth century, England led the world in the production of fine lead crystal. In 1745, however, this came to an abrupt end when the Glass Excise Duty was enacted. Since this law taxed glass by weight, it severely inhibited the production of heavy lead crystal and made it impossible for England to compete with France, Bohemia and Ireland.

English glass manufacturers suffered under this tax for one hundred years. When the law was finally repealed in 1845, the glass industry began to flourish. One of the great signs of England's recovery was the building of the Crystal Palace for the Great Exhibition in 1851. Almost one million square feet of glass was used in its construction. Within its grand walls, glass objects of every kind, shape and origin were displayed.

English manufacturers were quick to imitate the successful styles and techniques of the French factories displayed at the Exhibition. Soon millefiori weights were being produced by factories in London and Birmingham.

Whitefriars concentric millefiori

Bacchus close packed millefiori

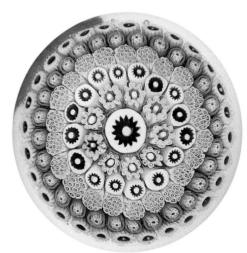

Whitefriars close concentric millefiori

31

Whitefriars close concentric millefiori

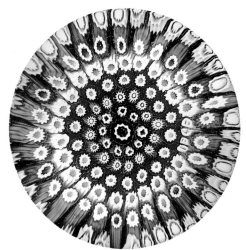

Whitefriars close concentric millefiori

Whitefriars close concentric millefiori

Whitefriars

"By 1700 there were eleven glass factories in London, including Whitefriars, making lead glass. The first products were tableware, especially the increasingly popular clear glass decanters used for the fashionable port wine. 'At the Flint Glass House in White Friars,' runs an advertisement of 1710, 'are made and sold by Wholesale and Retail, all sorts of Decanters, Drinking glasses, Crewitts, etc., or glasses made to any pattern of the best Flint, as also all sorts of common Drinking Glasses and other things made in ordinary Flint Glass at reasonable rates.'"
(Paul Hollister, *The Encyclopedia of Glass Paperweights*)

It is generally believed that the Whitefriars Glass Company of London was constructed about 1680, shortly after the great fire of London. This location provided for easy transport of sand, clay and coal for the furnaces, and other materials needed for the making of glass.

The glass company was named for the white-robed Carmelite monks who had lived in a monastery at the site of the factory until 1538. In its early years Whitefriars primarily produced glass tableware, especially clear glass decanters and drinking glasses.

In 1834 James Powell (1774–1840), a glassmaker from Bristol, purchased Whitefriars and renamed the company James Powell and Sons. This name was used until 1962 when, after the death of the last of five generations of Powells, the company name reverted to the original Whitefriars Glass Ltd.

Some glass historians believe that Whitefriars made its first millefiori paperweights in 1848. However, others counter that there is no record of paperweights having been made by Whitefriars before the 1930s. Whitefriars did not exhibit paperweights with its other products at the Great Exhibition in 1851, where the company was presented an award for its fine crystal. The case for early Whitefriars paperweights is not closed. Modern scholars will continue to study the records and actual weights until it can be decided whether Whitefriars did, in fact, make paperweights in the nineteenth century.

Early weights supposedly made by Whitefriars are characterized by the use of a concentric millefiori spacing scheme. Generally these weights had very low, shallow domes and wide bases. The millefiori canes were usually quite close to or actually touching the bases. Labels found on some of these early weights bear the logo of the white-robed monk and the words "Whitefriars" and "Powell's English Glass." A few early Whitefriars weights include date canes; the majority do not.

The company continued making paperweights until 1981. Then the business, which included the color library, millefiori canes and the name and logo, was sold to Caithness Glass. Caithness is now producing weights under the Whitefriars name.

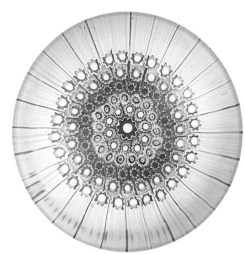

Whitefriars close concentric millefiori

Bacchus

Bacchus chequer

> *"The introduction of these ingenious and pretty ornaments from Bohemia has induced some of our glass manufacturers to turn their attention to the production of similar objects. We have seen a large number of home manufacture, which, for beauty and variety of colour, are equal to the best imported; and in design are superior to them. Mr. Bacchus, an eminent glass manufacturer of Birmingham, has produced some that deserve special notice for their novelty and elegance."*
> (*Art-Union Monthly Journal of the Arts* (1849), quoted by Paul Hollister in *The Encyclopedia of Glass Paperweights*)

Birmingham was the main English center of glassmaking activity during the 1800s. One of the factories in operation during that time was Bacchus, Green & Green of the Union Glass Works, which was founded in 1818. In 1833, the company name was changed to George Bacchus & Co. George Bacchus died in 1840. The next year the firm name was changed to George Bacchus & Sons. In 1858 it was retitled Bacchus & Sons.

The glassworks, which initially specialized in domestic glassware and plate glass, began experimenting with fancy Venetian-style glass and paperweights in the 1840s. "Letter weights," as they were sometimes called, were never more than a minute part of the company's production, but did attract attention.

Most of the weights made by Bacchus are large, usually more than three inches in diameter.

Sandwich clematis

Sandwich poinsettia on jasper ground

Mount Washington rose with buds

AMERICAN FACTORIES

The history of paperweight making in America is documented more fully than production in France. Three American glass-houses stand out as the principal paperweight producers in these early years: the New England Glass Company of East Cambridge (NEGC); the Boston & Sandwich Glass Company at Sandwich on Cape Cod; and the Mount Washington Glass Works of South Boston and New Bedford. All three factories were founded by Deming Jarves, an enterprising Boston merchant. They all also drew from the same group of skilled craftsmen, many of whom began as European apprentices. Occasionally, these craftsmen even swapped millefiori rods (knowingly or unknowingly). Therefore, it is sometimes difficult to distinguish between the paperweights at each factory, though each glasshouse had a distinct history and reputation.

Many of the early American weights are imitative of the French style—scrambled, millefiori, nosegay and fruit weights in clear glass or on latticinio grounds. The canes of the American antique weights are less complex in structure than those in the French antiques. However, American makers soon branched off, making a distinctive variety of lampwork subjects, including roses, poinsettias and fruit motifs.

Like so many developments that were transported from Europe to America during the seventeenth and eighteenth centuries, paperweight making arrived in the United States perhaps a decade after its appearance in Europe. American glass factories became interested in paperweight production after seeing the European weights on display at the Crystal Palace.

The first dated American paperweight that has been authenti-cated was produced by the New England Glass Company in honor of the Crystal Palace Exhibition in London in 1851. The piece was a flat, hexagonal-shaped plaque with impressed intaglio portraits of Victoria and Albert in the clear crystal base. The following year, 1852, seems to be the beginning of serious produc-tion of paperweights at New England Glass Company, as numer-ous examples of weights with that date are in existence.

Paperweight design and production continued intermittently in the United States into the early part of the twentieth century.

New England Glass Company

NEGC leaf weight

"Already in its first year it was called 'one of the most extensive flint glass manufactories in the country.' Two flint furnaces and twenty-four glass-cutting mills, operated by steam, and a red-lead furnace capable of making two tons of red lead per week, enabled them to produce every variety of plain, mould, and the richest cut glass, as Grecian lamps, chandeliers for churches, vases, antique and transparent lamps, etc. for domestic supply, and exportation into the West Indies and South America."
(Paul Hollister, *The Encyclopedia of Glass Paperweights*)

The New England Glass Company (NEGC), also referred to simply as "Cambridge Glass," came into being in 1818. It grew out of the purchase at public auction of two Cambridge firms: the Boston Porcelain & Glass Company and Emmet, Fisher & Flowers. Four partners, among them Deming Jarves, who became general manager, incorporated in 1818 as the New England Glass Company of Lechmere Point, East Cambridge, Massachusetts.

The company soon became one of the leading flint glass producers in the country. Workers there began experimenting with decorative glassware and their extensive product line included every variety of plain, engraved and pressed glass. By 1850 the factory's work force had grown to 500 men, working around the clock.

NEGC crown

The New England Glass Company produced paperweights from about 1850 to 1880. Its first known weight was a piece commemorating the Great Exhibition of 1851, which featured intaglio portraits of Queen Victoria and Prince Albert. In 1856 the company exhibited weights at the Franklin Institute's twenty–fifth exhibition in Philadelphia and at the Charitable Mechanics' Association exhibition at the Mechanics' Hall in Boston. The fact that the company included paperweights in its commercial display indicates that weights were not regarded as incidental production items.

There were several talented craftsmen who worked with NEGC over the years. John Hopkins and his father Thomas made the company's first medallion weights in 1851. Thomas Leighton (1796–1849) and five of his seven sons worked at NEGC. In order to evade the British law that forbade glassworkers from leaving

NEGC blown fruit

35

NEGC bouquet

NEGC fruit on latticinio

NEGC blue poinsettia on latticinio

the country, Leighton had left his home in Birmingham on the pretext of traveling to France on a fishing trip. William, the most creative of Leighton's sons, discovered an original formula for the popular ruby glass. He also produced some of the factory's most highly prized double overlays.

The most renowned craftsman at NEGC was Frank (François) Pierre (1834–1872), an Alsatian who served as an apprentice for Baccarat before working at NEGC in 1849. Pierre was known for creating the blown pear and apple fruit weights. Pierre's lamp-work fruit weights and millefiori pieces had a great influence on paperweight making in America, particularly on the work of William Gillinder, who also worked at NEGC at that time.

The 1870s brought severe problems for NEGC, involving labor disputes, rising fuel costs, and fiscal mismanagement. In 1878 the firm was leased to William L. Libbey. When he died in 1883, his son Edward continued to manage the business until 1888, when he closed down the New England plant and moved it to Toledo, Ohio. The modern facility of Libbey-Owens-Ford is the present-day survivor.

Sandwich

> *"The subscriber informs his friends and the publick that his Flint Glass Manufactory in Sandwich, is now in full operation, and is ready to receive and execute orders for any article in that line—particularly Apothecaries, Chemical and Table Wares. Also, Chandeliers for Churches and Halls, Vase and Mantle Lamps, Lamp Glasses and all other articles usually made in similar establishments."* (An 1825 advertisement signed by Deming Jarves during the first months of operation)

In 1823, Deming Jarves, the general manager or "agent" of the glass operations at the NEGC, inherited $25,000. He went to Pittsburgh to learn more about the manufacture of fine pressed, cut and engraved glass. In 1825, he left NEGC to form his own glass factory, the Sandwich Manufacturing Company. In 1826, the firm was incorporated and renamed the Boston & Sandwich Glass Company, known to the glass world simply as "Sandwich." Jarves became general manager of the operation and remained with the company for thirty-three years, until 1858.

The history and growth of Sandwich closely parallels that of NEGC. The two companies competed and maintained a friendly rivalry, similar to that between Baccarat and Saint Louis, until both firms closed down in 1888.

Most of the paperweights made at Sandwich during the early years were scrambled weights, some bearing the dates 1852 or 1825 or both. The 1825 date has usually been considered an error involving reversal of the last two figures in 1852.

Deming Jarves left Sandwich Glass in 1858. He formed the Cape Cod Glass Company for his son John; but John died in 1863 before the company was incorporated. Deming Jarves continued with the business on his own until his death in 1869.

In the later years of Sandwich Glass, Nicholas Lutz, one of the most famous of all American glassworkers and paperweight makers, was associated with the company. Lutz was born in Saint Louis, France in 1835. At the age of ten he became an apprentice at the Saint Louis factory. He later traveled throughout Europe gaining experience as a glassworker and paperweight maker. He worked at a number of glassworks, including those in Murano. Along with six other glassblowers, Lutz migrated to the United States, where he worked for the NEGC for two years. In 1869, just before Jarves's death, Lutz began working for Sandwich, where he remained until the company closed in 1888. After that he was employed by the Mount Washington Glass Company, and later by the Union Glass Factory. Lutz is best known for his filigree glass, French-style paperweights, and fruit and flower weights.

Like NEGC, Sandwich experienced labor problems and financial difficulties during the late 1880s. Finally in 1888 the firm closed, despite efforts by the board of directors to keep it operating.

Mount Washington Glass Company

In 1837, Deming Jarves started yet another glass manufacturing operation in South Boston—the Mount Washington Glass Company. Jarves started the company for his son George, who was twelve years old at the time. Unfortunately, George died in 1850 at the age of twenty-five. After the death of Deming Jarves in 1869, the firm changed hands many times.

Sandwich striped double clematis

Sandwich weedflower

Sandwich wheatflower

Mount Washington rose and butterflies

Gillinder concentric millefiori

Millville crimp rose

Not much is known about the paperweights made there, but it is known that master glassblower Nicholas Lutz worked at Mount Washington between 1892 and 1895, perhaps creating many of the unusual and outstanding magnum paperweights and plaques for which the company is known. Of these, the most famous is the Mount Washington rose. Only a small number of these weights are known to exist.

Gillinder

"In 1861 my grandfather founded his own company in Philadelphia and during the 1860s made a great many different types of paperweights at the Gillinder factory. I had an opportunity to visit the factory and found a room that was not being used. In the room was a box of rods that he had used, probably 200 pounds or more. These were of a great variety—stars, millefore, figures, etc. Unfortunately, fire a short while later destroyed the room and its contents."
(Letter written by James Gillinder of Gillinder Brothers, Inc., Port Jervis, to Evangeline Bergstrom on June 30, 1948; quoted by Paul Hollister in *The Encyclopedia of Glass Paperweights*)

William T. Gillinder was born in England in 1823 and spent his early life in the Birmingham area. Gillinder, who began working in a glasshouse when he was eight years old, became the secretary of the National Flint Glass Makers Society of Great Britain by the time he was twenty-eight.

In 1854, at the offer of a job as gaffer for NEGC, Gillinder moved his family to the United States. When they arrived, however, he found that because of a slump in business, he was offered a less important position. Gillinder moved frequently with his wife and children, working at various glass factories, and making an unsuccessful attempt at setting up his own glassworks in Baltimore, Maryland. In 1861, he purchased an old bottle factory in Philadelphia and started what was first called the Franklin Flint Glass Works. It eventually became known as Gillinder & Sons.

William Gillinder made many different types of paperweights. Canes from Gillinder & Sons were considered representative of American millefiori canes.

Millville

> *"But the most ingenious paperweights at Millville were those upright scenes derived from iron or steel dies (as described above) and made by Michael Kane. In paper-thin colored glass pictures as delicate as if they had been etched, Kane shows a hunter and his dog flushing a covey of quail, a yacht, a clipper ship, or the American eagle (white against a translucent red ground) in a superb series of vignettes that sets the pulse to beating with chauvinistic nostalgia. These large, clear, heavy, handsome weights come plain, footed, on pedestals, and occasionally, as with the clipper ships, in pairs that were probably used as mantel ornaments. One can sense the vestige of Bohemian engraving through flashed glass, but these vertical colored pictures, that catch the light from behind, are strictly and completely American."*
>
> (Paul Hollister, *The Encyclopedia of Glass Paperweights*)

Millville crimp rose

Some of the best-known American paperweights were produced at Whitall Tatum & Company, in Millville, New Jersey. Commonly referred to simply as "Millville," the factory was first established in this location by James Lee and associates in 1806. It changed hands several times until 1844, when it was acquired by the Whitall brothers.

Millville frit eagle

Over the years the glassworkers created a variety of distinctly American paperweight designs and motifs. Most commonly they included inkwells containing spotted, umbrella-like lilies; design profiles in powdered glass (frit weights); motto paperweights bearing slogans such as "Home Sweet Home"; and presentation weights depicting colored glass pictures and scenes. Michael Kane is the only person definitely known to have made the upright sailboat, dog flushing a covey of quail (very rare), horse, and eagle paperweights at Millville.

Millville became famous chiefly for the upright roses made by Emil Stanger, Marcus Kuntz, John Rhulander, Ralph Barber, and later Emil Larson. Called the "Millville Rose," these weights contain a three-dimensional upright flower set in clear glass, sometimes set on a pedestal base.

Millville umbrella

How Paperweights Are Made

Materials

The making of a paperweight begins with the quality of the glass. It is essential that a glassworker have the ability to control the weight, color, feel, and overall effect of the glass being used.

The basic ingredients in all glass are the same: sea sand and inorganic salts, such as soda and potassium nitrate. In high-quality colorless glass, called crystal, lead oxide is added to give brilliance and weight. Certain metallic oxides are added to obtain colored crystal. These colors are made according to exact formulas specific to the factory.

To begin to produce glass, all the components are mixed together and melted in large fireproof clay pots inside a furnace. These fragile pots must be replaced periodically due to cracking and corrosion. After the raw materials have been heated to temperatures exceeding 2600° Fahrenheit, the molten mixture is "boiled," or stirred, to eliminate any imperfections in the melt and make the glass more homogenous. At this point, the glass is a red-hot liquid. As it cools to a working temperature, it can be manipulated and shaped with an array of special tools.

Sand: the raw material of glass

Changing the furnace

◀ *Lampwork tools and materials*

Techniques

Paperweights may be constructed in two general ways depending on the kind of equipment used. Some glassworkers or factories have furnaces to produce molten glass; others use torches or lamps to melt a slug of premade glass. Many aspects of the process are the same. First the millefiori canes or lampwork figures are created and arranged on a metal template. They are then heated to just below the melting point to avoid cracking when hot glass is added. A metal collar is placed around the arrangement. The glassworker gathers a small ball of molten glass on the end of a long iron rod, rolling it and working it into shape on a metal plate or marver. The red-hot glass is then lowered into the collar to pick up the preheated design.

If the worker has a furnace, the canes or design elements are placed in the template face down by the first gather of glass, which forms the ground of the paperweight. If the glassworker uses a lamp or torch to make the decorative elements, they are placed in the collar in an upright position. Then the first gather flows in on top of the design, sometimes aided by a vacuum. The glass is blocked and shaped.

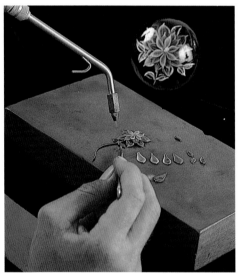

Tools and materials for making paper-weights

Assembling a lampwork flower from its elements; the finished weight is shown above

Finished lampwork components

42

The piece is then reheated in the glory hole, which can be an opening in the heating oven or a separate fabricated unit. This step allows for careful reheating of the glass. Another gather of clean molten glass is then added to form the dome of the weight (in the case of furnace work) or the ground (in the case of lampwork). The lampworker must now attach a second pontil rod to the base and remove the original one.

From here the final blocking process begins. The worker rolls the pontil rod back and forth across the arms of his glassworking chair so that the still-soft glass will not sag or become misshapen. During this process the weight is shaped and smoothed with a wet wooden block or contoured pad of wet tissue or newspaper to form a smooth dome. While the glass is still in the pliable state, tongs are used to form a slender neck at the base of the weight. When the piece has cooled significantly the worker gives a sharp tap to the pontil rod. The weight breaks off and falls into a bed of sand or a special device constructed to hold it.

The next step is to gradually and evenly cool the weight in an annealing oven. This process is extremely delicate. Sometimes the gathers of glass and the design elements within a weight cool at different rates, causing the piece to shatter and crack.

Developing a torchwork design

Shaping the finished weight

Reheating weight in glory hole

Forming a foot on the base of the weight

Molds for millefiori canes

Arranging millefiori canes on templates

The final stage of the process is grinding and polishing. At this point the pontil mark, the scar made when the weight was separated from the pontil rod, is ground and polished. Often the dome or sides of a weight can be faceted, that is, cut with a flat or rounded grinding wheel to form decorative windows for enhancing the design.

A paperweight is hand crafted during each step of its creation. Even if many weights of the same design are made by a glass factory, each one is different.

Millefiori

The Italian word *millefiori* means "thousand flowers"; it is used to describe decorative elements that make up some of the most popular paperweight designs.

The first step in making a millefiori paperweight is the production of a variety of glass rods or canes. The glassworker gathers molten glass from the furnace and works it into shape on a marver. If color is desired the gather is rolled in glass powders or color is gathered over the molten glass. It is then pressed into an iron mold and allowed to cool. The glass is then removed and another gather of molten glass is added. The piece is again worked on the marver and pressed into a mold of a different shape. This process can be repeated several times to build layers of colors and designs within a cane.

At this stage the rod may be about three inches in diameter and six inches long. The piece is reheated and another glassworker attaches a second pontil to it. The two workers quickly move apart, stretching the heated rod until it is pencil-thin and up to thirty feet long. The design within the rod, no matter how intricate, is accurately miniaturized. However, only a small portion of the elongated rod is stretched evenly enough to be used. This choice section is sliced in tiny pieces that become the canes within a paperweight.

After the canes have been made they are arranged in a pattern on a metal template, heated with a hand torch, and encased in glass.

There are several types of canes. Simple canes are of specific shapes such as circles, stars, cogwheels, arrows, and honeycombs. A complex cane is made by bundling simple canes together, then heating and stretching them again to form a new cane. Other types of canes are silhouettes, portraits, spirals, and signature and date canes.

Fusing canes together in glory hole

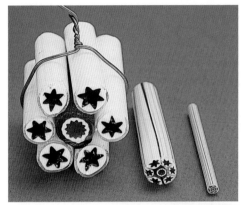

Three stages of a complex millefiori cane

Nearly completed millefiori design

Millefiori weight and a variety of canes

45

Contemporary Paperweights

Paperweight Revival

"Little by little, this art passed from fashion after 1860. The first French author on paperweights, Madame Yolande Amic, believed that the overabundance and poor quality production from second-class factories contributed to the decreasing popularity of the paperweight, and finally to the loss of their manufacturing technique. She has concluded that 'This small world of familiar objects, ornaments of the noiseless residences of our forebears, was rendered out-of-fashion, dead forever, doomed into oblivion at the bottom of some dust closet of specialized museums.' These weights, born in the Victorian era, favored by Queen Victoria and Empress Eugénie, fell out of fashion into a surprising and meaningless obscurity."
(Gérard Ingold, *The Art of the Paperweight—Saint Louis*)

A period of almost a hundred years separated the glorious classic period of paperweight making from what is now considered the revival period of the art in the 1950s. In October 1951, a magnificent millefiori paperweight was found in the cornerstone of the old parish church at Baccarat, which had been severely damaged during World War II. The weight, which included an 1853 date cane, contained 233 millefiori canes. The piece was made by Baccarat's master craftsman, Martin Kayser. The discovery of the "Church Weight," as it has come to be called, helped rekindle interest in paperweight making and collecting.

◀ *Ed Nesteruk silver-veiled design, Chris Buzzini braided stem bouquet, Ken Rosenfeld daffodil and lilac bouquet, Jon and David Trabucco branch of acorns and berries, Randall Grubb double overlay bouquet, David Salazar ocean ecosystem, Parabelle Glass nosegay on upset muslin*

One of the driving forces behind the paperweight renaissance was importer and enthusiast Paul Jokelson, who in the early 1950s approached the factories of Baccarat and Saint Louis and urged them to revive the art. Glass artisans were then faced with the enormous task of rediscovering the nearly lost techniques.

The first contemporary weight made by Baccarat was a sulphide. Because they had no remaining records of the millefiori technique, it took several years of research and experimentation before its craftsmen finally succeeded in producing millefiori weights in 1957. By that time the company had already mastered sulphide production. Baccarat's first successful sulphide commemorated the coronation of Queen Elizabeth II in 1953.

Baccarat craftsman Jean Benoit began working on lampwork-style paperweights in 1968. In the early 1970s Baccarat added lampwork weights to its contemporary line. In 1974 they began producing a lampwork collection for each year.

The process of producing sulphides remained a mystery to Saint Louis glassworkers until a nineteenth-century piece could be broken open and examined. In 1953 Saint Louis issued its first twentieth-century paperweight—a sulphide commemorating the coronation of Queen Elizabeth II. Between 1952 and 1955 the factory produced a few lampwork and millefiori pieces.

International interest in paperweights soared after the 1950s, and scholars began researching information on the field. In 1952 Paul Jokelson established the Paperweight Collectors' Association, which publishes an annual *Bulletin.*

It is important to acknowledge that certain talented individual artists had been making paperweights before the revival of the 1950s. These artists include Paul Ysart, Charles Kaziun and Frances Whittemore. In their own spirited and tenacious way, they form a bridge between the antique and modern weights.

As soon as modern paperweights became commercially successful, more glass factories joined Baccarat and Saint Louis in producing them. Cristal d'Albret, Perthshire, Whitefriars, and others began utilizing traditional techniques and classical motifs as well as exploring new possibilities in design and technology. Today, a whole new generation of paperweight artists adds vitality and innovation to this classic art.

Albert Schweitzer overlay sulphide

General Douglas A. MacArthur flash overlay sulphide

Menachem Begin and Anwar Sadat sulphide

D'Albret

As with Baccarat and Saint Louis, Paul Jokelson also encouraged Cristalleries et Verreries de Vianne of France to begin producing paperweights. The glass factory, which was founded in 1918 by Roger Witkind, began producing sulphide weights under the name "Cristalleries d'Albret" in 1967.

George Simon, a well-known engraver for the French Mint, was the first artist to create sulphide cameos for the factory. His pieces include the first four sulphides produced at d'Albret: Christopher Columbus, Franklin Roosevelt, King Gustav VI of Sweden, and John F. and Jacqueline Kennedy.

The engraver Gilbert Poillerat, who had worked extensively with sulphides at Baccarat, began making sulphides for d'Albret in 1968. Poillerat was responsible for most of the sulphides in the d'Albret series.

D'Albret sulphides are produced in both regular and overlay editions. All weights of the same subject are finished with identical faceting and the same color or color combinations. Weights are signed on the base with acid-etched letters arranged in a circle reading "CR. D'ALBRET—FRANCE." The cameo within the weight is signed on the edge of the bust with one or more of the following: the name of the subject, the date the sculpture was made, and the name or initials of the artist.

Rick Ayotte

"As you become more proficient in paperweight making, the motif starts to develop a feeling of color harmony, a scene in nature, a moment in time which is enclosed forever in crystal. I realize I am known mostly for my birds, and I will continue to make that a major part of my life's work. However, as a lover of nature and glass, and having been blessed with insatiable curiosity, there are many ideas that I enjoy working on, such as butterflies, animals, flowers, leaves, trees, earth, sky, reptiles, fish and water. Recently I have started down a new and very exciting road—three-dimensional subjects. This avenue shows promise to be the most exciting and, of course, the most challenging of my career."

In the world of paperweights, Rick Ayotte is known as the "bird man" of glass. His fascination with birds goes back to childhood where, in his native Nashua, New Hampshire, he charted migratory bird groups and carved life-size birds out of wood. Since the late 1970s, he has been making ornithologically accurate paperweights. His skill and artistic expression have now grown to include naturalistic settings that lend realism to the birds they surround, and three-dimensional still-life paperweights of incredible accuracy and complexity.

Ayotte studied at Lowell Technological Institute and later worked as a scientific glassblower in Nashua. In 1970 he started his own business, Ayotte's Artistry in Glass, which specialized in solid crystal and hollow glassware gifts. While working as a scientific glassblower, Ayotte became acquainted with Paul Stankard, who worked at the same company. Stankard encouraged him to try his hand at paperweight making. Ayotte found paperweight making a creative challenge as well as an opportunity to combine his skill and expertise in glass with a longtime interest in ornithology. In 1978 the first Ayotte weights appeared on the market.

Scarlet-chested parrot, golden-fronted leafbird, barn swallow chasing insect, red-breasted bluebird in flight, wood thrush in flight, pair of bluebirds, crissal thrasher

Chrysanthemum bouquet, Illusion fall bouquet, Eastern bluebird and wild roses, frog on a lily pad, desert scene with quail

In his earlier weights, Ayotte's birds were set in simple surroundings. His later work grew to include intricate foliage, berries, flowers, butterflies, nests, and the use of color grounds. His use of lampwork flowers and vegetation is extensive. He has developed a compound layering technique, which gives a sense of depth to his work. Many of his birds and flowers are now upright and three-dimensional. These weights are very difficult to create, involving hours of tedious lampwork.

Ayotte has recently completed a series of complex glass sculptures which he calls "Illusions." Eight years of planning, preparation and experimentation were necessary before their successful execution. In these pieces, the central design is viewed upright. Due to the precise contouring of the glass, a circle of translucent color at the back of the piece is seen as a halo of color around the finger facets—thus the optical illusion. They are limited to no more than fifteen pieces each.

Ayotte produces paperweights in editions of from ten to seventy-five pieces. He signs his work with an engraved "Ayotte" plus edition number and size on the base.

Scattered millefiori on lace

Baccarat

"There is something magical about the name Baccarat. To the uninitiated it conjures up visions of gambling and Monte Carlo, and for those who collect paperweights it conjures up visions of some of the most beautiful flowers and millefiori decorated weights that the world has ever known."
(Peter Lazarus, *Collectors' Guide* magazine, February 1970)

In 1953 paperweight collector and connoisseur Paul Jokelson suggested that Baccarat experiment with making sulphides. Their first attempt, which was a piece based on Dwight D. Eisenhower's campaign medal, was unsuccessful. But the experiment proved to the craftsmen that encasing cameos in glass was possible. That same year the factory produced its first successful contemporary sulphide commemorating the coronation of Queen Elizabeth II of England. The paperweight proved extremely popular and led Baccarat to the production of a long series of sulphides.

Snake on rocky ground

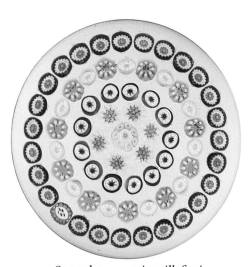

Spaced concentric millefiori

Lampwork flower encircled by millefiori

Because Baccarat had no records of the millefiori technique, it took several years of research and experimentation before they succeeded in producing millefiori pieces in 1957. With the advice and help of Francis Whittemore, Baccarat craftsman Jean Benoit mastered the technique of lampwork-style paperweights, and in 1974 began an annual lampwork collection. These weights present a variety of designs using flowers, fruit, or animals on clear and colored grounds. In 1970, Baccarat revived the Gridel silhouette canes, which had been considered a trademark of the factory's millefiori work during the nineteenth century. In the contemporary series, a large Gridel cane is surrounded by smaller Gridel silhouettes and various arrangements of other canes.

All contemporary Baccarat weights bear an acid-etched seal that includes the words "Baccarat, France" and the outlined forms of a goblet, decanter and tumbler. An interior date/signature cane and the number of the item are often included in special limited edition weights. Most Baccarat sulphides are inscribed on the edge of the bust with one or more of the following: the artist's name, the year the sculpture was created, and the subject's name.

Rose on latticinio

Thomas Jefferson sulphide

Preparing setup for Gridel weight

Gridel deer with 18 small Gridel canes

53

Ray Banford cabbage rose bouquet, fancy-cut basket with iris, single cabbage rose with bud

Ray Banford

"Ray's wife Ruth instilled her love of glass in him, and years later this interest led him to Adolph Macho, an old South Jersey tank glassblower. After watching Adolph make a few paperweights, Ray was inspired to try his own hand at glass work, but with a torch. He started working in his garage with a butane torch, together with his son Bob. Like a father who buys his young son a set of electric trains only to play with them himself, Ray gave Bob a gas oxygen burner for graduation and took advantage of every opportunity to use it when Bob wasn't around. After three years of self-instruction he produced a salable miniature weight, and from that point on advanced to regular-sized weights in a large variety of designs." (Ruth Kaplan, 1985–86 PCA *Bulletin*)

The Banford family comes from Vineland, New Jersey, an area rich in glassmaking history and tradition. Ray Banford's father knew Emil Larson, the originator of the famous crimp roses. Ray had worked as an antique dealer for many years and often did business with paperweight makers Pete Lewis and John Choko.

After viewing Macho's work, and a subsequent visit to The Corning Museum of Glass, Ray and his son Bob set up their own paperweight studio in Hammonton, New Jersey in 1971.

Ray's paperweights include bouquets of lampwork flowers, as well as paperweight buttons and pendants. Occasionally Ray and Bob have produced "combination weights," in which lampwork elements made by both craftsmen are encased in a single weight.

Most of Ray's work is identified by a cane with a black "B" on a white ground; however, many of his early weights contain signature canes in a variety of color combinations.

Bob Banford

"I have always been fascinated by antique French weights. My work tends more towards the classic French style in my use of color, design and overall flow of the weight. There is a certain line, a rhythm to these classic weights which I in turn try to impart in my weights. I don't copy nature per se; *my flowers are stylized. I would rather make something that hasn't been seen before."*

Bob Banford upright bouquet with torsade, striped snake, six-flower bouquet, flowering vine with double overlay, fancy-cut book with cross of leaves, bouquet within a cut basket

Top row: Lilies-of-the-valley by Bob Banford, bouquet by Bobby, iris bouquet by Ray, four-flower bouquet by Ray and Bob, two-blossom bouquet by Bobby, trellis of morning glories by Bob.

Second row: Daffodil bouquet by Bob and Bobby, double iris by Ray, pair of blossoms by Bob, cabbage roses by Ray, four-flower bouquet by Ray and Bob.

Third row: Dahlia by Bob, cross of leaves by Bob, pansy bouquet by Bob, floral handcooler by Bob, single flower with buds by Bob.

Bottom row: Salamander by Bob, stem of cabbage roses by Ray, striped snake by Bob.

Upon finishing high school, Bob Banford worked as a scientific glassblower for a year and a half. He soon began demonstrating novelty glasswork and, in his spare time, experimenting with paperweight making.

In 1971 Bob and his father Ray began seriously producing paperweights. Since that time they have worked together in a small studio behind their family home in Hammonton, New Jersey. They share ideas and techniques, but work as independent craftsmen and have each developed distinct and individual styles. Bob was the first lampwork artist to produce compound weights.

The Banfords have produced distinguished basket and gingham weights whose intricate faceting and cutting are integral to the design. Most of their complex cutting is done by Ed Poore, who is considered one of the best paperweight cutters in America.

Bob Banford's classic-style paperweights include lampwork flowers, intricate upright and flat bouquets, bumblebees, dragonflies and salamanders. Each of his weights contains a signature cane made up of a red "B" on a white ground surrounded by a blue rim.

Bobby Banford

"After meeting Bob and learning about paperweights, I discovered that working with glass would be a way for me to finally let loose my creative self. I've always loved art, and I wanted to be a cartoonist or perhaps go into advertising. I am so fortunate to have Ray and Bob as teachers. They are both so patient. My love of nature and the ocean has been an endless source of ideas and inspiration."

The third member of the Banford team, Bobby Lee Sanford married Bob Banford in 1984. She began spending her spare time at the Banford studio learning how to make clear glass animals and ornaments. Shortly thereafter she started working in the studio full-time creating glass paperweights. Her favorite subjects are floral motifs, undersea designs and holiday scenes.

Bobby Banford's other artistic talents include drawing, painting, ceramics, calligraphy and various crafts. One of her weights was chosen for the Wheaton Museum Collection in 1988.

Her weights are signed with a script "B" in turquoise on a white ground, surrounded by a ring of turquoise.

Stylized bouquet

Holiday weight with snowman

57

Long-spurred violets

Buzzini's sketch of violets

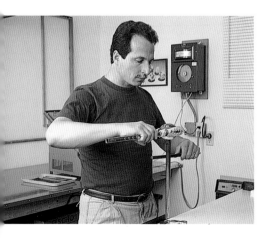

Buzzini signature cane

Chris Buzzini

"Because I studied and observed lampwork for years before I began it myself, the basic process and techniques came together easily. But now, after five years of lampworking, it is becoming clearer that perfection is always unobtainable. Some of the strong points of my paperweights are use of color, attention to detail, and sense of design. Yet of greatest importance is the awareness that realism has become the most essential part of my work. Now it has become even more important for my flowers to be accurate. My early pieces had some recognizable flowers, but now I try to have all the components as accurate as I can within my current abilities and the materials available to me."

Christopher Lee Buzzini was born in Yosemite National Park in 1949. The magnificent natural beauty of his birthplace was to have a great influence on his future career, giving him a strong connection to nature and a love of color and detail. He began college as a student of architecture. While taking a drawing class he discovered the ceramics department, which led him to the school's glass program. He became fascinated with the medium and entered the glass department at Chico State University.

Buzzini set up a glass studio in his home so that he could experiment on his own. In 1972 he became a small-interest partner in the newly formed art glass studio of Orient & Flume. From there he went on to work at several other prominent art glass studios in California, including Lundberg Studios and Correia Art Glass. He also had the rare opportunity to work with a patron, Gaylord Evey, who was instrumental in setting up a studio for him in New Jersey. Also during this time, glass artist Pete Lewis openly demonstrated his lampworking skills, and along with James and Nontas Kontes, offered advice on obtaining and setting up equipment. Through these various work experiences Buzzini expanded his knowledge and gained precision in his technique.

From 1983 through 1986 Buzzini worked as a paperweight artist at Correia Art Glass in southern California. He was primarily designing and creating torchwork weights, although during that time he also began studying and experimenting with lampwork techniques on his own.

In the fall of 1986 he set up his own studio in southern California where he could be free to formulate and create the detail and realism that his personal aesthetic demands. He began making the superb botanically accurate weights for which he is now known. They include specific wildflowers, orchids, roses and lilacs. He now limits his yearly edition pieces to editions of twenty-five or forty.

Chris Buzzini and his family have moved from California to Oregon. Buzzini believes that the influence of this area, which abounds with natural beauty, will have an even greater impact on his work than do his memories of Yosemite. Buzzini is the only artist who includes a full name and date in a cane within the design. He also signs and dates his pieces in script on the side of each weight.

Aster and China rose bouquet; azalea, crocus and butter lupine bouquet; desert scene with desert flame blossoms; crown vetch; paphilopedilum orchids; faceted spring bouquet of apple blossoms, morning glories, heather and wild blue flax

Lilac and China rose bouquet

59

Snake coiled atop a golden globe

Correia Art Glass

"Glass is perhaps the most versatile media, permitting the artist an almost limitless combination of form, color and dimension. It has extraordinary paradoxical qualities. While hot, glass is a fluid medium of expression, yet it is in this facile state only a few moments while it is out of the furnace. Once glass starts to cool, it becomes brittle and clumsy to work with. During its few moments in its molten state, one must deftly translate creative impulses into shapes, which become irreparable parts of the final piece. At every state in its creation, in the mixing of the chemicals, in blowing and shaping the glass, and finally in the decorating of the piece, one is forced to test simultaneously the limits of imagination, concentration and technical control."
(Steven Correia)

Founded by Steven Correia in 1974, Correia Art Glass is located in southern California. The studio has since become world-famous for its art nouveau and art deco designs, iridescent color, and exceptional quality.

Steven Correia was born in San Diego on February 14, 1949. He showed an early interest in art and was encouraged by grade school and high school teachers. He later attended San Diego State College and the University of Hawaii, receiving an MFA from Hawaii. Originally interested in sculpture and ceramics, his work with three-dimensional mediums led him to glass work.

Frosted window weight
with hummingbird

Early Correia weights were mainly Tiffany-style iridescent surface decorations. Later weights utilized lampwork designs, characterized by floral, animal and aquatic scenes. Chris Buzzini created paperweights for Correia from 1982 to 1986.

Correia Art Glass is now run by Correia family members. Steven has moved on to producing large-scale laser performances, and glass sculptures using cold glass techniques.

Frosted window weight with heron

60

Randall Grubb

"In my mind, this combines the best of all possible worlds. I buy the best glass, which is absolutely clear and as beautiful as it can be. Then I can work exclusively on the artistic end. Hot glass is such a wide open medium. There is tremendous potential in it. We are using new techniques that are virtually unexplored."

Bouquet with double overlay, branch of white plum blossoms, branch of mauve plum blossoms with double overlay, branch of mauve plum blossoms

Randall Grubb was first introduced to hot glass in the University of Southern California's art department. He fell in love with the hot glass process for its seemingly unlimited potential. Grubb wrote his senior business plan on opening a hot glass studio. As part of his study he worked for Correia Art Glass in southern California as an equipment builder. Such in-depth exposure to the many facets of hot glass gave tremendous experience to the young and talented Grubb; it also gave him his introduction to paperweights. At the studio he met paperweight artist Chris Buzzini, who greatly influenced his future career, giving him guidance and training in the art of making paperweights. Since

Various bouquets, including roses, lilacs, knotweed and stylized flowers

Grubb was employed as an equipment builder, he was able to roam the studio freely, observing and asking questions.

Chris Buzzini oversaw the first couple of weights made by Grubb. Buzzini had a great deal of technical experience behind him, while Grubb had experience in equipment building and had ideas to offer in that area. His first weights were made with torchwork procedures, but he found they lacked the three-dimensional capability he wanted. When Grubb met Larry Selman at an antique show in southern California, he saw lampwork weights for the first time and was thoroughly fascinated. Shortly thereafter he began experimenting with this technique.

He initially constructed individual lampwork elements and included them in glass pieces such as perfume bottles. By the time he had acquired the equipment necessary to encase the elements in crystal, he was already proficient at making lampwork motifs.

Grubb currently designs and creates his own line of lampwork paperweights in his Oregon studio. Because he pulls his own canes to obtain exactly the right shades, his use of color is exceptionally delicate and satisfying. Floral weights are his first love and main focus. Many of his weights contain full, colorful bouquets surrounded by high domes. His bouquets have become increasingly more complex in color and design.

The wine grape bouquet weights represent an entirely new concept for Grubb. They were completed after a lengthy development process with much experimentation in both color and design. Fifteen prototypes preceded the finished designs, each containing six clusters of different colors for perfect shading and hues. He is also one of the few artists using the complicated overlay and double overlay techniques, often with special cutting to highlight his original designs.

Randall Grubb engraves his name and the date on the side of each weight, and now includes a signature cane in his work.

Harold Hacker

"I was born in Weston, West Virginia, and on my eleventh birthday I visited a local glass plant for the first time. I was amazed to see the workers making a variety of shapes from the molten glass, and when I was offered a job in the factory I accepted. My first assignment was to carry champagne glasses to the lehr for the slow cooling process. I was fascinated by the molten glass and every morning and evening I was practicing taking glass out of the furnace and controlling it on the blow pipe. My interest attracted the attention of an experienced glassblower, and during a visit to his home I was introduced to the art of creating figurines formed by melting beautiful colored rods and tubes over a very hot torch. I thought at that moment 'I must learn this art.'"

During the late 1930s Harold James Hacker moved from his native West Virginia to the Los Angeles area and began working in technical glass. After serving in the armed forces in World War II, he established a glass concession at Knott's Berry Farm, a Los Angeles amusement park. He built up a successful business that lasted twenty-three years making intricate glass figures, including a carousel and a coach with horses, which he produced by manipulating colored and clear glass rods over a torch.

In 1966 Hacker read about a paperweight that had sold at auction for more than $14,000. The article suggested that paperweight making was a lost art and that no one could duplicate the antiques. With his extensive glass and lampworking experience, he set up a small furnace and workshop and began making lampwork paperweights in his spare time. Hacker's weights include flowers, fruit, snakes, salamanders and many other kinds of animals.

Turtle

Harold Hacker died in 1989. His weights are signed in script with a diamond-tipped pen in one of three ways: "H. J. H.," "H. J. Hacker," or "Harold J. Hacker," with the full signature indicating the higher quality weight.

Robert Hansen

A professional lampworker from Bridgeport, Michigan, Robert Hansen specializes in glass animals and figures. The brother of Ronald Hansen, he has also created some paperweights, most notably his lily-of-the-valley weight, which is fashioned after a famous piece by Clichy. Robert Hansen signs his weights with a full signature in script on the base.

Ronald Hansen

"For what manner and in what way does a weight communicate with you? Does the arrangement and color bring fond memories? Does it make you reminisce? Is some color in it like a favorite article of apparel you once prized or like the color design in one of grandmother's favorite vases? Does it bring to mind a calm sea on a pleasantly remembered journey, or a sunset on the desert? Possibly the flower reminds you of your favorite garden or a bouquet received that brought much pleasure. It would be hard to visualize a fine weight that could arouse any emotion other than pleasure and enjoyment."

As a boy growing up in Minnesota, Ronald Hansen came upon two itinerant craftsmen—possibly immigrants from Europe—using a charcoal fire and improvised bellows to fashion glass ships out of soda bottles sawed in half. This was his introduction to glass.

As a glassblower, he specialized in the manufacture of neon tubing. His interest in antique glass and the creative potential of the medium led him to paperweight making. Using only torches, he experimented with many different paperweight motifs, especially those popular in antique French weights.

His paperweight subjects include snakes, fruit and flowers. His successful weights are very collectible; unfortunately, weights flawed in production were not consistently destroyed and sometimes made their way into the market.

Ronald Hansen died in October, 1986. His son, also named Robert, began making weights at the age of thirteen. Ronald Hansen signed his weights with a blue and white "H" cane.

Ronald Hansen yellow clematis, three cherries, nosegay, blue clematis, lily-of-the-valley, crimp rose

"J" Glass (John Deacons)

John Deacons, a skilled designer trained at the Edinburgh College of Art, formed "J" Glass in 1979 in Crieff, Scotland. The company derived its name from the enigmatic "J" signature cane found in certain nineteenth-century Bohemian weights. Deacons chose this same mark to honor the unknown creator of those ingenious weights and to identify his own skillful creations. The company produced paperweights in the classic style until it ceased operation in 1983.

"J" Glass paperweights include floral, insect and reptile designs in lampwork as well as patterned millefiori motifs. Produced in limited editions of not more than 101 pieces, "J" Glass paperweights are signed with a blue "J" encircled by date numerals in red, green and blue contained within a single cane.

In 1990 John Deacons began making limited edition lampwork and millefiori weights again. His latest weights are signed with a "JD" cane and a date cane.

John Deacons lampwork flower with radiating canes, pansy on latticinio, rose on latticinio, dogwood on latticinio, crown

Pedestal crimp rose, miniature pedestal rose, silhouette, spider lily perfume bottle, perfume bottle with crimp rose

Charles Kaziun

"Even from a distance, a 'Kaziun' is recognizable because of his use of rich colors, which the artist feels is of primary importance. Close inspection of his pieces reveals the high quality of his workmanship and his obvious respect for perfection, lessons learned early in his career. After almost fifty years in the business of glass, Kaziun continues to create his exquisite works of art. Although his quest for excellence severely limits the number of pieces he feels are good enough for sale, it has also put his works on a par with those old French paperweights that were his ideal and inspiration so many years ago."
(Doris B. Robinson, 1983 PCA *Bulletin*)

Charles Kaziun, one of the pioneers of paperweight making, has been working since 1939 to rediscover the lost techniques of the French glass factories. His work includes a wide range of millefiori, lampwork and crimp flower paperweights, and related items.

He began his career by patiently observing a family of glassblowers demonstrating lampwork at the annual fair in Brockton, Massachusetts when he was just a boy. Through persistence he was allowed to work with them, eventually creating his own offhand pieces.

Double overlay rose

He was employed as a scientific glassworker during World War II, striving always to unravel the mysteries of glass. When he was introduced to Emil Larson and the Millville rose, his true life's work began. After almost four years and several thousand dollars worth of experimentation, Kaziun perfected his version of the crimp rose. Kaziun's roses, which are smaller than their Millville counterparts, are today highly valued by collectors.

Over the years Kaziun has created a wide range of flower weights, incorporating the pansy, hibiscus, dogwood, convolvulus, and in one of his most popular pieces, a miniature spider lily. His work also includes many superb perfume bottles.

Kaziun has produced excellent spaced and patterned millefiori on colored grounds which are often flecked with gold. His millefiori weights often include silhouette canes of his own design. He perfected a swirling latticinio cane and a brilliant two-sided torsade. Many pieces include gold foil butterflies and bumblebees and the characteristic 14-karat gold "K" signature. Early weights contain a millefiori "K" signature cane which is integrated into the design.

Snake on mottled ground

Millefiori with torsade on gold-flecked ground

"Sunbonnet Sue"

James and Nontas Kontes

The Kontes brothers, James and Nontas, began working with glass in 1939 at a small glass factory in Vineland, New Jersey. In 1943 the two formed their own business, the Kontes Glass Company, which specialized in the production of laboratory and research glass.

In the early 1970s, they began to collect paperweights. Fascinated with both antique and modern weights, they turned a small section of their factory into a paperweight studio. Their motifs include flowers, fruits, snakes and composites.

Each brother works independently and marks his pieces with an individual cane. Nontas's weights are marked with a bright yellow "NK" cane in clear crystal; James's signature cane has a black "JK" monogram on white ground with a ring of yellow-on-red star canes encased in pink.

Dominick Labino

In 1963, after working for thirty-five years in the glass industry, Dominick Labino began blowing glass for the first time. He brought to his work in art glass the skills and experience he had gained in glass research and technology. His free-form designs, swirled colors and carefully planned air sculptures constituted a unique and inventive approach to paperweight making.

Kontes strawberries on upset muslin

Born in Pennsylvania, Labino studied at the Carnegie Institute of Technology and the School of Design of the Toledo Museum of Art. Shortly before retiring, he built a workshop in back of his home with the intention of continuing his research into glass production. He began studying the production and control of color and form in art glass.

Labino used no crimps or molds to form the motifs that make up his paperweights. His designs include free-form flowers, coiled snakes on iridescent grounds and abstract designs in clear or colored glass. Many of these designs are surrounded by swirling veils of color achieved by adding silver to the melt.

Dominick Labino marbrie weight

David Lotton crown

Labino, who died in 1987, influenced an entire generation of glass artists. His work as a paperweight maker marked a new direction in contemporary paperweight design. Examples of his works are owned by more than twenty museums in the U.S. and Europe, including the Smithsonian Institution and The Corning Museum of Glass.

Labino's signature and the year are engraved on the base of each of his pieces.

Charles and David Lotton

A fascination with iridescent glass led Charles Lotton of Lynwood, Illinois to build a small workshop with a furnace and an annealing oven. There he began to experiment with glass and glassblowing. In 1973 he started working full time to produce paperweights and vases in the art nouveau style. Many of the designs he used were taken from Egyptian, Oriental, Islamic, and Greek themes. One of his greatest accomplishments was the discovery of the formula for mandarin red glass.

Paperweights made by Charles Lotton are not finished on the bottom and show a rough pontil scar near the script signature.

*David Lotton "Dua flora"
iridescent surface design*

David Lotton began helping his father, Charles, in his art glass studio at the age of ten. While working as his father's assistant, he began experimenting on his own. By 1975, when he was fifteen, he was producing his own paperweights.

David Lotton makes weights with floral motifs as well as crown designs. All his pieces carry his signature and the date inscribed on the base.

David Lotton

David Lotton vine of iridescent flowers

Lundberg Studios

"What I like about glass is its spontaneity—it is just so alive. Every morning you open the ovens and there are pieces and completed works inside. When I first started working in glass I became really addicted to it; I could hardly sleep at night. I'd find myself up at 3 or 4 in the morning, handling those pieces while they were still hot." (James Lundberg)

Carol Trevis, Steven Lundberg, Daniel Salazar, and James Lundberg

James Lundberg founded his studio in Davenport, California in 1973. The studio is now a partnership of the two Lundberg brothers, James and Steven. Lundberg Studios first became known for its iridescent glass and art nouveau style. Later its clear-encased weights with floral, bird, butterfly and seascape motifs marked the emergence of a new form of paperweight. Most recently James Lundberg has developed a series of "Worldweights" that are extremely accurate depictions of earth and its atmosphere.

James Lundberg first studied glassblowing at San Jose State University during the late 1960s. Involved in ceramics from an early age, he worked his way through school as a technician in

Iridescent weight

Worldweight by James Lundberg

71

Daniel Salazar yellow rose of Texas, Daniel Salazar peony, Steven Lundberg underwater scene, Daniel Salazar crane, Daniel Salazar cherry blossom, Daniel Salazar Pacific tidepool

the ceramics department and attended the first class in glassblowing at SJSU. He became interested in the composition of glazes, and later glasses, and is today considered an authority on the chemistry of colored glasses. He now formulates and melts all his own materials.

In 1971 a graduate tour took him to Europe to continue studying glassmaking techniques. On returning, he stopped in New York and was introduced to Tiffany art glass. He was struck by both the beauty and the appropriateness of this art nouveau style, and began to develop similar iridescent colors and patterns. Today Lundberg Studios is the foremost replicator of Tiffany-style blown glass.

In 1972, with the encouragement of paperweight dealer L. H. Selman, James, aided by his brother Steven, began applying his iridescent glass techniques to paperweight designs. The success of this direction was overwhelming and helped advance their business from a backyard workshop to a professional studio. Within months Steven began making his own creations. Over the years he has worked in all aspects of glass at the studio, but for the past decade he has concentrated his skills entirely on crystal encasement. It was Steven's original idea to combine pre-lampworked parts with his torchwork designs, creating a major breakthrough in both realism and three-dimensionality.

Daniel Salazar began as an apprentice in 1975. From childhood Danny demonstrated a strong interest in art. Since 1981 he has produced his own designs and is now considered a master paperweight artist. Both Steven and Daniel have collaborated with in-house cutter and engraver Carol Trevis to produce a very limited number of specially faceted pieces.

In 1974 Lundberg Studios began producing an entirely new form of paperweight. Called the California Paperweight Style (or torchwork), it represented a hybridization of two antique styles—the art nouveau "icepick" technique and the lampworking procedures found in French paperweights. By using a surface-mixing hand torch, the artist could apply and manipulate color additions with considerable delicacy. By utilizing more sophisticated canes, layering and pre-lampworked inserts, the technique has become a major new direction in paperweight making. This new process is the culmination of almost twenty years of development and is mainly the work of Steven Lundberg and Daniel Salazar, with notable contributions early on by James Lundberg, Mark Cantor, David Salazar and Chris Buzzini.

In 1989 James Lundberg developed the Worldweight, which now accounts for fully half of all the production at the studio. The Worldweight has consistently been chosen for prestigious awards. This earth paperweight, created using a complex powdered glass drawing and several layers of specially formulated glass, represents another new style pioneered by Lundberg.

Lundberg Studios continues to be a leader in developing new designs and motifs. Examples of their work are included in almost every major museum and private glass collection. Each weight is signed with the studio name, artist's name, date and registration number.

Steven Lundberg fuchsia

Daniel Salazar beta fish

Steven Lundberg dahlia

Iridescent fish and stingray

Frog near lampwork blossoms

Coiled snake on rocky ground

William Manson

"I believe versatility is the key word for me, and the desire to create outstanding designs often overrides the quest for realism. Paperweight collecting is all about happiness, satisfaction and appreciation. Combine all these things and you will have achieved the ultimate aim of paperweight makers and collectors everywhere."

William Manson's career in glass began in 1966 when he joined the Caithness Glass Company as an apprentice glassblower. Under the strict supervision of master glassblower Paul Ysart, he was introduced to the art of making glass paperweights. He left the company with Ysart in 1970 and began an even more intensive training which lasted for four years and gained him a tremendous amount of experience in the field. When he returned to Caithness in 1974 he took over the designing of limited edition weights, using his own unique style.

Manson's pieces include lampwork flowers surrounded by garlands of millefiori canes, salamanders set on rocky grounds, fish, and swans.

Manson weights are signed with a signature/date cane and numbered on the base. Each design is limited to 150 pieces.

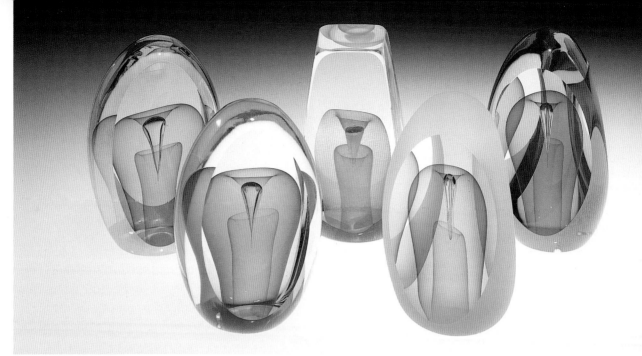

Abstract silver veiled designs

Ed Nesteruk

"I feel strongly that art objects made of glass should fully utilize the fine qualities of glass. 'Why glass?' should be obvious. The main fascination I have is with its transparency. Three-dimensional transparent objects with internal forms are absolutely magical."

Edward Nesteruk of Pittsburgh, Pennsylvania entered the art glass world with a solid technical foundation in Chemical Engineering from Penn State University and seventeen years of experience working for chemical and glass companies. He founded his own glass studio in 1980. During the years of his engineering career, his research and development was devoted to finding new methods of coloring hot glass surfaces. Several patents have been issued in his name, all related to glass coatings. This vast knowledge of coloration has proven to be his trademark.

Nesteruk's glass pieces have been veiled in a tremendous array of colors, including aqua, brown and orange. Veils are produced by coloring clear glass surfaces and gathering more glass over the colored surface, giving them a light, gossamer quality. Nesteruk's pieces are made of 24% lead crystal. Each piece is hand-ground and polished in five separate stages. The facets are added to visually enhance the interior glass veiling. Each of his pieces is signed and dated in script on the bottom.

Michael O'Keefe

"The design is very satisfying. It has a certain amount of move-ment to it, yet it is calming—like a mood inside a piece of glass. These shapes are so aesthetically satisfying that they cannot be improved upon. They are complete. There is nothing that I could add to make them any better than they are."

Michael O'Keefe of Seattle utilizes the process of silver veiling in his paperweights. He learned this technique while studying at the Center for Creative Studies in Detroit, where he received his BFA in photography and first started taking classes in glassmaking. The silver veiling process involves melting together silver and glass. By reheating the glass the silver is drawn to the surface where the design is developed. The piece is then encased with additional glass and the outside is fire polished.

The soft and fluid exterior shapes of O'Keefe's work are meant to reflect what he has created in the interior of the piece. He uses the outside as a frame for viewing the form within, and the resulting harmony and balance are extremely effective.

O'Keefe's work was greatly influenced by the time he spent in Japan while in the Navy. During his three years there, he gained an appreciation and love for the Japanese aesthetic which is very much reflected in his glasswork. His pieces involve a high degree of craftsmanship and yet manage to maintain an overall feeling of elegance and simplicity.

Michael O'Keefe stopped making paperweights in 1990. His weights are signed and dated on the bottom with a diamond stylus.

Silver veiled gradations

Free-flowing seashell design

Orient & Flume

"The first house where we blew glass in Chico, California was located between Orient and Flume Streets. We liked the sound of a combination of the two names and chose it for the personal meaning to us. However, the word orient also means a pearl of great beauty, value and luster. Flume is derived from a French word that means to flow. Our glass designs are flowing and fluid. So the words orient *and* flume, *in effect, define the glass."*

In 1972 Douglas Boyd and David Hopper opened a small glass-blowing studio in Chico, California. The two artists, who had taken part in some of the earliest college glassblowing classes offered on the West Coast, received master's degrees in glass from San Jose State University. After graduation they traveled throughout Europe, studying antique glass and glassmaking techniques.

Orient & Flume has grown from a two-person operation to a glassworks with a staff of twenty people. It can be described as both a studio and a factory, in that it has the required furnaces and can dependably produce glass in quantity; the facility runs eight colors regularly and has the capacity for twenty. It is still small enough to allow each artist the chance to work and create as an individual.

The company developed its reputation producing brilliant iridescent glass paperweights with art nouveau motifs and elaborate surface decoration. When Boyd and Hopper began experimenting with formulas, iridescent glass had not been produced for almost half a century. There were no artists living who were familiar with the technique; the original formulas took years of research to develop. But in the process, they learned the techniques and technical information needed to make their own glass, while also gaining a strong background in glass history and design. Early paperweights were made using the technique of torchwork, where molten threads or dots are applied to the surface of a piece and then manipulated to create a pattern. Later work included clear-encased lampwork weights.

Orient & Flume produces its own glass and creates its own colors. A studio approach is used for most pieces, in that a piece is created from start to finish by one person. However, the shop process method is used in iridescent pieces, so that the gathering, decorating and polishing are each done by the person most skilled in that area.

Since 1982 Douglas Boyd has been the sole owner of the company. Orient & Flume weights are signed, dated and numbered.

Iridescent spring bouquet

Canada goose

Parabelle Glass

"My grandmother had a paperweight, and from early on I was interested in them. When I developed my studio I decided to figure out how to make millefiori weights. There's more mystery for me in millefiori than in lampwork—and at that time there was no one in this country doing that type of work. I had no technical information about the process, except in the most general terms, and that added to the challenge. I also had many people tell me that I could not do it—and that's the wrong thing to say to me." (Gary Scrutton)

Gary and Doris Scrutton of Parabelle Glass in Portland, Oregon are the only studio artists in the United States concentrating exclusively on the production of millefiori paperweights.

Gary first began working with glass in the 1940s. He started as an apprentice after high school, learning general glassworking techniques such as beveling, etching and mirror silvering. He later started his own studio which specialized in stained glass. In 1983 he sold the business to his two sons, and he and Doris set up a small studio in the back of their home where they began making millefiori weights.

Spaced concentric on carpet ground, quatrefoil garland on moss ground, close concentric millefiori with pansy center, lampwork blossom on upset muslin, close concentric millefiori piedouche, Christmas wreath on lace ground

With only the most general information available, Gary spent the first year in his new studio experimenting with the making of glass and the development of techniques. He worked diligently to overcome problems involving equipment, design and the making of colors and canes.

Doris Scrutton primarily creates the setups for the millefiori designs. She is also the walker in stretching the millefiori canes. In contrast to many studio artists, Gary makes all his own colors, purchasing his raw materials from a local supplier. He has also developed a highly sophisticated glass studio with computers regulating the temperatures of the furnace and the glass formulas. With these methods, the Scruttons are able to maintain a high level of quality control over their finished weights.

Clichy has been a great influence on the Parabelle paperweights in terms of style, color and design. Their contemporary use of classical motifs is especially evident in their close packed millefiori, garlands and basket designs.

Parabelle weights are signed "PG" in a cane within the design.

Close concentric rings of stars, concentric millefiori with central Clichy rose, intertwined garlands on upset muslin, spaced millefiori garland, spaced concentric millefiori with central pansy, close packed millefiori

Perthshire Paperweights

"If we've got a secret to all our success today, it is that rarely can a person come along and say 'That's mine—I made it.' Other hands have been involved. In other words, we are really doing what the traditional famous factories in glass and china did— developing a team and a factory name."

Perthshire Paperweights was founded in 1968 by Stuart Drysdale, a Scottish country lawyer and businessman, who died in 1990. The factory is located in Crieff, a small farming community in central Scotland.

Drysdale, who first became familiar with paperweight manufacture while managing Vasart Glass and Strathearn Glass, was introduced to the beauty and technical sophistication of antique French paperweights through an article in an American magazine (*Woman's Day*) in 1967. He became intrigued with the idea of creating paperweights equal to those made during the classic period.

In 1968 Drysdale and the master glassblowers of Strathearn left that company and formed Perthshire Paperweights. For the first two years the operation was located in an old schoolhouse that had been converted into a makeshift factory. Although paperweights had been produced in small numbers at Strathearn, they were extremely simple in design. When Drysdale became aware of the rich history and sophistication of fine antique paperweights, he determined to rediscover the nineteenth century techniques.

In 1971 Perthshire Paperweights moved into a newly constructed modern factory on the outskirts of Crieff. They are now one of the few factory-size operations in the world devoted exclusively to making paperweights and paperweight-related items. About three-quarters of a ton of glass is now produced each week at Perthshire. The company employs about thirty craftspeople who work together designing and producing paperweights. Millefiori

Downtown Crieff

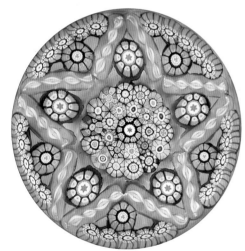

Patterned millefiori star

Hollow weight with interior kingfisher, branch of apples, lampwork ▶ bouquet on swirl ground, magnum lampwork flower, butterfly in stave basket, double overlay Scottish thistle, lampwork flower on honeycomb ground

Completed weight with lampwork elements

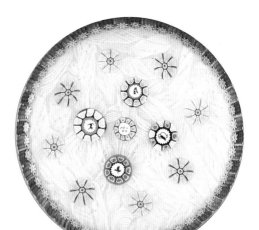

Scattered millefiori on muslin

and lampwork designs are created by the glassworkers themselves, and experimentation is encouraged.

A high standard of excellence is maintained at the Perthshire factory and paperweights can be rejected at any stage of the paperweight-making process if they are flawed in any way. A final review is made after the weights have been annealed. Only about thirty percent of the pieces which are started make it through the many levels of examination. Rejected weights are saved until the end of each week and then destroyed by a covering of molten glass scrapings from the furnace.

Perthshire regularly issues three types of paperweights: the special yearly collection; regular limited issues; and decorative weights. Perthshire's yearly collection is made up of new designs created for a specific year, produced as limited editions, and never repeated. These pieces include a cane containing the "P" initial or a "P" cane with the year of issue.

Tudor rose

Crown with lampwork flower

Christmas candle

Patterned millefiori with latticinio twists

Three-color swirl

Perthshire's regular limited issues are weights produced in small quantities for a specific number of years. Some of the pieces are signed alphabetically, with the letter "A" representing 1969, the first year of production, "B" 1970, etc.

Perthshire's decorative weights are considered to be the finest weights of their type on the market. In a great variety of sizes, they display patterned millefiori designs that are often concentric rings divided by a wheel and spoke arrangement of thin spiral canes. These colorful attractive weights help finance the production of the time-consuming limited editions.

Besides these three types, Perthshire also occasionally makes one-of-a-kind pieces. In addition to paperweights, they produce perfume bottles, tumblers, door knobs and other fine quality glass pieces which include millefiori and lampwork designs.

Lampwork bouquet with dragonfly

Corn and chiles, tomato vine, vegetable garden, pumpkin patch, ripe raspberries

Ken Rosenfeld

> *"I have always been attracted to the size and shape of a paperweight, to the intimate qualities of the small object. It is a small precious piece that fits in your hand. It is very basic. I feel the round shape is very primal; this aspect has always fascinated me. The inner space has a lot of magical powers. The inside imagery is brilliant, bright and seductive; yet it is untouchable. You can look all you want but you can never touch those flowers. They are captured under that pristine glass—sealed in that environment for eternity."*

Ken Rosenfeld specializes in detailed lampwork designs in the traditional French style. His weights include a variety of flowers, floral bouquets, fruit and vegetables.

Rosenfeld was a graduate student in ceramics at Southern Illinois University when he first became interested in glass. After college

84

he returned to his native California and started a small glass studio with a partner, an endeavor that lasted one year. He spent the next five years at Correia Art Glass, working on their extensive production line and developing his own ideas. He next worked as a scientific glassblower, gaining experience with sophisticated glass technology and a higher level of precision.

Rosenfeld first became interested in paperweights while attending the 1980 PCA convention in New York City. He was greatly impressed by the exquisite selection of antique French paperweights on display; but it was the extraordinary work being done by contemporary artists that inspired him most. He researched all available material on the subject of paperweights, and then began creating his own. When his first weights were offered for sale, the response was immediate and gratifying.

Rosenfeld's work reflects his skill as a craftsman as well as his accomplishments as an artist and designer. He creates his own glass rods so that the colors, so essential to his designs, are exact. What interests him most is the color and the liveliness of the design. While the technical aspects of quality and composition are very important, he feels that the color is most important. His strong sense of color is apparent in both his interior motifs and translucent color grounds.

Rosenfeld has moved from Southern California to Oregon, where he has set up a much larger studio with three furnaces. His weights are signed with an "R" cane; his name and the date are engraved on the base of each piece.

Cluster of cabbage roses

Clematis-type flowers on a carpet of blossoms

California poppies

Saint Louis

"Finally, in 1951, the shop supervisor nominated me for a thrilling assignment: try to remake, identically, nineteenth-century paperweights. I was eighteen years old when a long period of research and testing began for me. With the aid of Louis Lutz, the first rods were produced, and after a few weeks, the first paperweight reflected the light of day. . . . I knew many secrets remained, especially the one concerning the upright bouquet. Not until I saw an old bouquet broken in two was I able to recover the lost secret." (Paul Gossman, 1953)

Encased gingham overlay bouquet

In 1953, after a lapse of eighty-six years, Cristalleries de Saint Louis once again began making paperweights. The initial prompting came from Paul Jokelson, who at the same time had encouraged paperweight production at Baccarat and Cristal d'Albret. Paul Gossman, an energetic young glassmaker at Saint Louis, consulted with the older workers at the factory, then conducted test after test to rediscover the forgotten millefiori, lampwork and sulphide techniques.

In 1953 Saint Louis issued its first twentieth-century paperweight. This limited edition sulphide was made to commemorate the coronation of Queen Elizabeth II. Between 1952 and 1955 Saint Louis produced a limited number of paperweights (300–400) in addition to the coronation sulphide. Lampwork motifs included clematis, daisy, pansy, cherries, fruits and vegetables on lace; there was also a millefiori piedouche and a millefiori upright mushroom with overlay.

Bouquet within millefiori heart

Blown gilded lizard

Super magnum and regular size piedouches

In 1965 Saint Louis produced a faceted butterfly weight that utilized both lampwork and millefiori techniques, a snake weight, and an upright lampwork bouquet. In addition, the factory began production of a small series of sulphides.

Beginning in 1970, Saint Louis made a commitment to produce paperweights on a regular basis. Since then the factory has issued a set of limited editions each year. The technique, design, color and size of modern Saint Louis weights have their origins in nineteenth-century artistry. The company also produces a number of paperweight-related items such as handcoolers, candlesticks, newel posts, perfume bottles and pen holders.

In 1973 Saint Louis produced a super magnum piedouche, standing 9½ inches tall and weighing 55 pounds, that was the largest modern millefiori paperweight made; it was limited to eleven pieces. In 1991 four slightly smaller super magnum pie-douches were made. Each of these enormous weights took nearly a week to make, and at least another week to anneal.

Modern Saint Louis weights contain a cane with the date and the initials "SL." Each weight is produced as part of a limited edition and is accompanied by a certificate of authenticity.

Saint Louis factory worker

David Salazar

"In Henry Miller's Black Spring, *he alludes to things, places, instances that inspire a feeling of 'oneness,' an affirmation of one's being. The moment I read that passage, I knew that I could wholeheartedly relate to it. Sometimes it's the execution of a design, the application of a color that to most seems incidental, but to me it makes a world of difference. To the few visitors and students I get in my shop, I try to describe what a wonderful challenge it is to have worked with glass for the last eighteen years. It's still more than inspirational—it is my passion."*

In 1972 David Salazar sat transfixed as he watched the fascinating process of glassblowing for the first time. As Mark Cantor, James Lundberg's partner at the time, explained the process, Salazar projected what he would do if given the chance. With a limited background in scientific glass work and a strong desire to learn the magic art of blowing glass, he became an apprentice at Lundberg Studios.

*Ocean ecosystem with
outer marbrie design*

Translucent heart with gold hearts and vines

From the beginning Salazar's emphasis was in decorating. So in 1973, when Larry Selman suggested he concentrate on paperweights, the "door was opened." The early days flew by with a seemingly endless work load and a lot of after-hours experimentation. In the course of that year he combined his experience in scientific glass work and conventional glass methods with the new techniques he had learned to create original images.

Since 1985, when he opened his own studio in Santa Cruz, California, Salazar has used his personally designed furnaces to better suit his needs. The first two lasted three years before being devastated by the 1989 earthquake. Fortunately, he had been building a new furnace at the time, consolidating all the colors into one furnace. It is presently supplying all of his glass needs more effectively and economically, and has also inspired a new furnace design that will further consolidate the melting and annealing processes.

In this studio he formulates his design concepts, melts his own glass, makes his own colored glass, and pulls his own rods and millefiori. His uses the techniques of torchwork, lampwork and millefiori to create weights in a great variety of motifs and a remarkable array of unusual shapes. His style is similar to art nouveau, with flowing lines and designs often set in relief.

Salazar's paperweight techniques have been influenced by the French factories of Baccarat and Saint Louis, both in the effective use of millefiori and the combination of different molds. He uses the star mold in his work and has developed a combination of colors and molds to make a sea anemone used in his angelfish piece. He feels that working alone is a bonus to his technique and ensures that he has total control of each of his pieces.

David Salazar's weights are signed and dated in script on the bottom.

Undersea scene with angelfish, algae and shells

Surface design butterfly, blossoms and stars

Crescent moon and stars

Floral harvest compote

Rambling rose

Hummingbird and foxglove

Barry Sautner

"In sixteen centuries only a handful of glass artists have been able to reproduce the diatreta of the ancient glass artists. Barry Sautner now stands not only head and shoulders above all others but in our opinion has surpassed the ancients in the beauty of his creations. Already Sautner has created more diatreta than all the ancient examples known. Sautner's technical skill and ingenuity, combined with his artistic ability, presage much for the future of this art." (Leonard S. and Juliette K. Rakow, *National Early American Glass Club Bulletin*, Spring 1986)

Barry Sautner, of Lansdale, Pennsylvania, began creating diatreta and insculpture paperweights in 1984. Diatreta is an extremely difficult and unusual process accomplished entirely by sandblasting of cold glass. The term is derived from the Greek word for openwork or latticework. A form of this technique dates back to the early fourth century AD; it was revived in this century by Frederick Carder at Steuben Glass. Only a few examples of this very fragile glass technique are found in museums today.

Beginning with cased blanks, Sautner uses fine sandblasting equipment to cut struts from the central crystal in order to support the cased layers. Feeling that the struts detracted from the design, Sautner experimented until he found a way to create a full diatreta with no supporting struts whatsoever. The design now supports itself.

Sautner also uses a sandblasting technique, called insculpture, that is his alone. By working through small holes in the base, he can create three-dimensional flowers and leaves in the center of the crystal.

In 1986 Barry Sautner opened Sautner Cameo Studio. The majority of his pieces are one-of-a-kind; the others very limited editions. Sautner's subjects range from the unusual and controversial to the sublimely beautiful. His weights are signed on the base with a diamond stylus.

90

James Shaw

"I like to think of my craft as a blending of science and art. I've read a lot and done a lot of research on the optics of glass. So instead of studying flowers and lampwork for paperweights, I'm studying the science of glass optics . . . I feel it's a different approach to a traditional medium—a modern approach— my own approach."

James Shaw began his career working in ceramics. In 1976 he was hired by Lundberg Studios to fire their kiln and quickly became fascinated with glassworking. At Lundberg Studios he was introduced to the delicate grinding and polishing technique that is so important to fine paperweights. He became well known in the paperweight world for restoration of weights, sensitively repairing damage and restoring pieces to their original shapes and facet patterns.

In 1985 Shaw started creating his own glass pieces. From the beginning his work showed skill and invention. His style and unique approach to form and shape have been greatly influenced by his extensive sculpting, cutting and faceting experience.

Shaw has expanded the art and technology of his work into a new dimension, creating a technique in which he laminates already formed, cold pieces of glass together, rather than fusing and manipulating the glass using heat. His lamination process is extremely slow and demands a great deal of precision. A complicated design can take up to two months to complete. Surfaces must be ground, put together, then extensively reground, using precision optical machinery. The flat surfaces are bonded with a specially formulated clear epoxy made for glass. Its brilliance and high index of refraction create a mirror surface for laminating.

Laminated block

Shaw is creating both symmetrical and asymmetrical pieces with complex internal designs and lamination. Futuristic in effect, these pieces use specialized glass originally made for scientific applications, but perfectly suited to Shaw's artistic purposes. His precision cutting and multiple faceting patterns create brilliant and provocative crystal sculptures.

James Shaw and his family now live in Oregon. He signs his weights in script on the side or bottom of each piece.

Geometric weight

Yaffa Sikorsky-Todd and Jeffrey M. Todd

"I make pieces that I myself would like to live with. My background as a painter led me to relate to clay forms as three-dimensional canvases; when I began blowing glass the dimension of motion and flow were added. After some experience, I have found that working in crystal glass allows me to use reflections and two sides of the piece visually interacting, as well as the pure optical qualities of the medium. I use nature as an impulse, blending my feelings and fantasies. I add and delete as I deem necessary to achieve a piece that will evoke a feeling of wonder and intrigue." (Yaffa Sikorsky-Todd)

Leafy tree with water and sky

Pond with cattails and butterfly

Yaffa Sikorsky-Todd was born in Tel Aviv. After completing her BFA in Ceramics at the Philadelphia College of Art, she worked as a studio potter for two years. She received her master's degree in glass at the Rochester Institute of Technology in 1977. Her master's thesis was written on fluorine opal glass.

Jeffrey M. Todd, from Philadelphia, Pennsylvania, majored in jewelry and glass at Southern Illinois University. He became interested in glass in the early 1970s, taking classes at SIU and at the Penland School of Crafts in metal-working and glassblowing.

When they first began working together in glass, they made goblets and perfumes. They next added lampworked flowers to the bottles which evolved into larger glass forms. When Yaffa and Jeff were invited to a paperweight show in 1987 they were encouraged to scale down their work to paperweight size.

In Yaffa's "Memories" series, vertical glass scenes are presented with multiple layers of imagery to create intricate, self-contained worlds. All the colors and crystal glasses are melted by Yaffa in the studio using formulas that she has developed over the last fifteen years. Yaffa and Jeff make all their own millefiori canes. Their collaborative "Natureweights" are traditional-style paperweights that incorporate elements of their natural surroundings.

Yaffa and Jeff have worked together for eleven years in their Burnsville, North Carolina studio. They exhibit nationally and internationally; their work is included in many private and museum collections. Each piece is signed and dated.

Gordon Smith

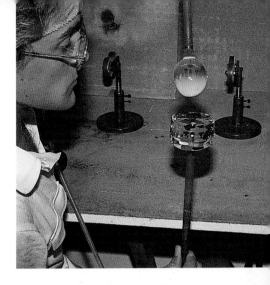

"As a glass artist, I feel blessed to have had the opportunity to express my love for the natural beauty that our planet has to offer us. My most recent artwork brings forth a beauty, awareness and understanding of coral reefs and the marine life that inhabits these reefs and underwater gardens. I feel that glass is the natural material through which to express these marine environments."

Gordon Smith first became interested in glassmaking at the age of fifteen while visiting a demonstration at Wheaton Village in 1975. The glassblower, noting his interest, encouraged him to enroll in the scientific glassblowing course at Salem College in Salem, New Jersey. In 1980 he began working for Kontes Glass, a scientific glassblowing firm owned by James and Nontas Kontes. The Kontes brothers devoted much of their spare time to making paperweights. Smith was fascinated and inspired by their work, and they in turn encouraged him to pursue his own interest in the art, and to work at Wheaton Village in the glass factory.

The Kontes brothers, the Banfords, and Paul Stankard all helped and encouraged Smith, but there were certain aspects of paperweight making that he had to discover on his own. By 1982, after much experimentation, he had broken through the technical barriers and was on his way to producing quality paperweights. His first successful paperweights included graceful lampwork floral designs. Fine detail is emphasized in these weights; each of his realistic raspberries has approximately fifty individual seeds.

Raspberry vine

Gordon first exhibited his "Marine Life" paperweights in 1986. The first designs were stylized fish in the traditional paperweight form. He used electric natural colors for the fish and incorporated his lampwork techniques to create complete aquatic environments with brightly colored coral reefs. Today these marine life paperweights are the main focus of his work. He wants his work to be appreciated both for its visual beauty and as representation of the ocean's fragile environment.

Gordon Smith now works in a small studio behind his home in Mays Landing, New Jersey. His work appears in museums all over the world. He signs his paperweights on the side with the initials "GES" and the date.

Lipstick tang

93

Paul Stankard

"It was an exciting breakthrough to go from paperweights to botanical blocks. In this new sculptural format I developed the concept of presenting what was both above and below the earth. When I translated this concept back to the paperweight format I discovered a new presentation which I called 'environmentals.' In the environmentals I explore life energy under the earth which is translated by 'spirits' or 'root people.' Presently, I'm incorporating this mythical imagery into both paperweights and the botanical series. It's interesting to me how both formats have influenced each other and the discoveries in one have directed my development in the other."

Paul Stankard, of Mantua, New Jersey, is perhaps the most prolific and accomplished paperweight artist working today. His skills have developed over thirty years of working in glass, drawing heavily on ten years of industrial experience. The Ware Collection of Blaschka glass plant models on display at Harvard's Peabody Botanical Museum was a major early influence on Stankard and heightened his interest in creating glass flowers.

Stankard's early work featured botanically accurate glass flowers focusing on detail, exact coloration, and the life cycle of the plant. He has a love of wildflowers, and many of his paperweights have intricate root systems that are detailed with as much care as the colorful blooms above the ground. He has recently translated his love of nature into poems intended to interpret the voice of a flower and heighten appreciation of his glass botanicals.

Throughout his career, Stankard has continued to expand the limits of the paperweight as an art form. He has conducted many studies, experimenting with color and composition to achieve his own personal interpretation of nature. In 1982 he developed his botanical series. These rectangular block-shaped sculptures break through the size and shape constraints of the traditional paper-weight. Inside they reveal delicate, finely crafted flowers as well as the hidden beauty of the plant's bulbs and root structures.

Many of the concepts Stankard developed in his botanical series are translated back into the traditional paperweight format.

Spring beauty cloistered botanical ▶

Peach blossom and bee, blackberry vine, Indian pipe botanical, experimental meadowreath and lilacs, wild roses

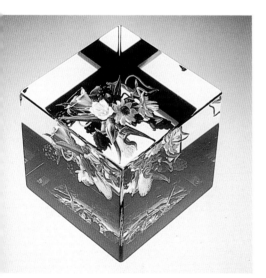

Bouquet botanical block

In the dome of these paperweights are delicate colorful flowers and vegetation crafted in his meticulously realistic style. Hidden beneath the ground on the underside of the paperweight is a completely different world—an environment with intricate root systems that are often anthropomorphic in form. Stankard calls these structures "spirits under the earth" or "root people." Spirits also appear in his cloistered botanicals. In these pieces, colored glass is laminated on three sides of the block.

During his career, Stankard has explored the limits of glass as an artistic medium. His extensive background in glass technology and his curiosity and drive as an artist have led him to create some of the finest and most original work being done in glass today. His works are represented in major private and public museum collections in the U.S., Europe and Japan. Stankard is currently on the faculty of the Pilchuck School of Glass in Washington, and Penland School of Craft in North Carolina.

Stankard's early paperweights bear a signature cane, an "S" or "PS" on the base or side of the piece. His recent work is signed in script and may also contain an "S" signature cane. All of his pieces are dated.

Goat's-beard with spirits

Flowering prickly pear

Tea rose bouquet

Trailing arbutus

Orchids

Kaleidoscope of flowers

Mix of fanciful flowers

Debbie Tarsitano

"As a painter I've transformed my sense of dimension, style and design into my paperweights. What I've learned from my painting is reflected in my weights. This perspective helps me especially with my scenic weights. I take a tremendous amount of time with each design and each setup that I make. I consider each paperweight as an individual work of art."

Debbie Tarsitano and her father Delmo Tarsitano saw their first glass paperweight at an auction in 1971. The purchase of that first paperweight and the enthusiasm it engendered led them to experiment with glass on their own. Del had taken a short course in glassmaking, and Debbie could make simple glass animals. Thus, with a borrowed torch and glass, they set up their first studio in 1976. Since those early days, with much trial and error, good instincts, and indomitable spirits, the two have become highly regarded paperweight artists.

Debbie's paperweights have been greatly influenced by her background in painting. She graduated from Hofstra University with a degree in art and painting. Her study of painting has influenced the style, color and design of her paperweights. She rarely makes more than a few examples of any design. She has worked in collaboration with the master engraver Max Erlacher, who worked at Steuben Glass for many years. First she creates an array of complex flowers, grasses and berries in the foreground; Erlacher then engraves a rural scene on the base of the weight.

Debbie Tarsitano creates her paperweight designs and setups in her studio in Massachusetts. She commutes to her father's studio in Long Island to encase her pieces. In 1990 she completed a dramatic work entitled "The Outstretched Hand of Liberty." The work comprises eight four-inch diameter plaques, each depicting a poignant scene of a family's journey from the old world and their quest for a better life in the new world. A marble base unifies the eight pieces into a single work.

Until 1980, her weights were signed with an initial "T" cane; thereafter her pieces are identified by a "DT" cane.

Bouquet with engraving by Max Erlacher

Delmo Tarsitano

"I'm basically a nature boy. That goes way back to when I was a little kid. We lived by the woods; there was swampland and water all around. I was always curious. I didn't care for spiders for a long time but now, as you can see from my work, I consider them my friends. My desert scenes have reptiles, cactus plants, everything. They keep evolving. I just keep going."

Delmo Tarsitano was born in northern Italy and grew up in the New York City area. He was first introduced to paperweights by seeing and purchasing an antique weight at an auction. He was fascinated enough to begin studying and collecting them, and eventually became an expert in the identification of antique paperweights.

In addition to appreciating the beauty of paperweights, Tarsitano took an interest in the technical aspects of paperweight making and began experimenting with making weights on his own. He produced his first successful paperweight in 1976. Three years later he and his daughter Debbie began making paperweights full-time.

"Earthlife" spider

Delmo has produced a series of salamander weights. He is also known for his "earth-life" weights—realistic presentations of spiders in their own natural environments. The grounds, creatures, and delicate flowers of his earth-life sculptures display complete mastery of the technical aspects of lampwork. With consummate skill and precision, he uses optical cutting to enhance each lifelike scene.

Tarsitano has introduced a new concept in paperweight encasement by replacing the conventional round dome with a rectangular shape. With this design there are no magnifications or distortions and the optics are vastly improved. Many of his new weights contain millefiori grounds.

Delmo Tarsitano's first weights were signed with a "T" signature cane. Weights made after 1980 incorporate a "DL" signature cane.

Coiled snake on rocky ground

Victor Trabucco

"For years the rose has been something that I've wanted to capture. When I started, the only realistic roses that I had seen were the crimp roses. But the crimp style has certain limitations; often the roses appear rigid, and you really can't include a crimp rose in a bouquet setting, just by the nature of how they are made. In my roses I've tried to create a delicate, satiny effect in the petals through my use of color. I use the color almost like a painter would—painting it on to achieve the shading effect. The challenge is to take something as hard and cold as glass and turn it into a very soft and delicate-looking petal."

Victor Trabucco of Buffalo, New York first became interested in glass in 1974. He began his career in glassmaking as a sculptor, quickly receiving award-winning recognition for his work. In 1977, after examining a number of French paperweights, he began experimenting with paperweight making. He was fascinated with the possibilities inherent in encasing delicate lampwork arrangements in solid crystal; after a year of trial and error he successfully mastered the technique. His work then focused on over-

Magnum lizard inspired by Pantin

Super magnum bouquet

Rose detail

Sculpture

coming technical problems in order to allow more latitude for artistic expression. He has found working in the paperweight format to be his ultimate challenge as a glass artist.

Trabucco's most recent paperweights are magnificent magnum-size pieces, four and five inches in diameter, containing full, beautifully sculptured flowers. Each paperweight displays a high dome of the highest quality crystal which increases the magnification of the blossoms and creates a lush, full-looking piece. Over the years he has developed a morning glory, camellia, daffodil and rose. These three-dimensional flowers are captured in full delicacy and realism. After years of experimentation, Trabucco was able to eliminate the bubbles and distortion which tend to occur when encasing some large lampwork setups. He is particularly proud of the rose technique that he has developed. Traditionally, the larger and more dimensional the flowers were, the thicker the petals had to be in order to withstand the encasement process. Trabucco has succeeded in capturing a realistic, fully open rose with separate delicate cupped petals. Many experts feel it is the finest example of a lampwork rose.

Another significant technical achievement of Trabucco's is the elimination of the line or seam which traditionally occurs in the glass of lampwork weights. He is the first American artist to succeed in floating an upright bouquet of flowers in the center of a weight without a division line beneath the flowers. In eliminating the line, the weight can be viewed from the side as well as the top with no obstruction.

Trabucco's magnum lizard weight was inspired by the rare Pantin reptiles. His main objective was not to merely duplicate their work but to pick up where they left off. He is the first maker to master the feat of encasing such a large subject in glass. Over five hundred pieces of cane scales are individually fused to the back of this magnificent reptile to add to its realistic appearance.

Today, Victor and his twin sons David and Jon work at Trabucco Studios in Buffalo. Victor's weights are signed with a "VT" cane; his signature and the date are inscribed on the side.

David Trabucco

Jon and David Trabucco

> *"Glass has always been a part of our lives; we grew up with it, and we realized from a very early age that we would be involved with it. We know how lucky we are. Our dad did all the experimentation, so we were able to start at a very high level. In another thirty or forty years, who knows what heights we will reach?"*

David and Jon Trabucco, twin sons of Victor Trabucco, grew up watching their father create splendid glass bouquets. In 1984, when they began producing their own lampwork weights, their father's years of experimentation enabled them to begin work at a much higher level of proficiency. They now produce their own line of paperweights, with David doing the setups and Jon handling encasements and faceting. Their weights show bright, well-balanced three-dimensional bouquets. They have recently added cherries and apples to the blossoms and buds in their paperweight designs.

David and Jon Trabucco sign their weights with a "T" cane and "Trabucco," the date, and their initials in script on the side.

Jon Trabucco

White blossom and bud spray

Whitefriars

The venerable London glassworks of Whitefriars produced fine glass continuously from the 1600s until 1981. In 1923 Whitefriars moved to Wealdstone, a nearby suburb.

Whitefriars was early known for its fine quality crystal tableware. Their color library, developed over a period of 300 years, contained the formulas and recipes for over a thousand colors, shades and tints. Classic concentric and patterned millefiori designs predominate in Whitefriars' modern paperweights. They also produced many commemorative weights, the first for Queen Elizabeth's coronation in 1953. Every Whitefriars paperweight contains its distinctive signature cane in the form of a white-robed monk along with a date cane.

In 1981 Caithness Glass of Scotland purchased the company's name and logo. Since then they have been producing paperweights under the name of Whitefriars; although these weights still include the traditional signature cane, they bear no similarity to earlier Whitefriars weights.

Variations of millefiori designs

Francis Whittemore

"I started blowing glass in 1938. I saw someone demonstrating the technique, got interested, and fooled around with it. Finally my father, who was a research chemist and teacher, said I needed better tools, so I went to a shop outside of Boston and purchased some decent equipment. Then I really went to work blowing glass. Actually, I never apprenticed anywhere. I got a lot of help, but essentially taught myself. I've done just about everything in the glass and scientific fields. I have an excellent technical background in glass, and a strong background in botany and biology as well."

What began with a childhood tour of the Blaschka glass flower collection at Harvard ultimately led Francis Dyer Whittemore, Jr. to a lifelong exploration of glass. He started blowing glass using the most rudimentary tools. By the time he entered college he had developed a successful business supplying goblets, decanters, and animal figurines to local gift shops.

Whittemore studied at Harvard University for two years before entering military service. After 1946, he spent sixteen years working as a technical glassblower developing and perfecting his skills in the field. Whittemore began making paperweights in preparation for teaching a class on decorative glassblowing in Salem County, New Jersey. Even with years of glassworking experience, it took him five years of experimentation to duplicate the deceptively simple-looking Millville rose. He created crimp weights with ten- and fifteen-petal roses in a variety of colors, set on pedestals. He also incorporated the rose into perfume bottles, glasses, and other small paperweight-related items.

Whittemore, who worked as a consultant to Baccarat for several years, started his studio in Lansdale, Pennsylvania, in 1968. He is well known for his beautifully designed lampwork flower weights set on clear and richly colored translucent grounds. His single-flower weights include the cornflower, pansy, jonquil, lily-of-the-valley, calla, daisy, tulip, crocus and poinsettia. He has also made a series of limited edition state flower weights.

Whittemore weights are signed with a "W" cane on the reverse of the motif.

Mushroom bouquet, fuchsia, columbine and bud

Paul Ysart

"Contrary to the practice of many collectors and dealers, Paul Jokelson promoted the virtues of fine antique and modern weights alike and refuted the criticism that this dual approach was detrimental to the beauty and exclusivity of the antiques and their craft. Instead, he asserted that the modern weights incorporated traditional techniques, not as reproductions, but as inspired and original 'works of art' in their own right. Paul Ysart's works were promoted both for their immediate delight and as 'antiques of the future'. By 1958 collectors were writing with pride and enthusiasm about the modern additions to their collections of nineteenth-century French weights: 'I've recently added two beautiful Paul Ysart weights: one has a lovely orange yellow butterfly on a soft orchid ground and is truly a meticulous work of art. The perfection of Ysart's work is evident and a joy to possess.'" (Alison J. Clarke, *Ysart Glass*)

Born in Barcelona in 1904, Paul Ysart is considered one of the most important contributors to paperweight making in the twentieth century. A paperweight artist since the 1930s, Ysart was among the first contemporary craftsmen to rediscover and refine techniques used in making weights.

Millefiori butterflies, lampwork flower and a garland of canes

Lampwork flower ringed by complex millefiori canes

Both Ysart's father, Salvador, and his grandfather were glass-blowers in Spain. Just prior to World War I, Salvador moved his family to France, where he worked as a master glassblower in Lyon, Marseilles and Paris. In 1915 the family moved to Scotland, where Salvador worked at the Edinburgh and Leith Flint Glass Works. It was there at the age of thirteen that Paul, Salvador's oldest son, began training as his father's apprentice. In 1922 Salvador was offered a position at Moncrieff Glassworks in Perth, Scotland, and he brought along Paul and his other three sons as apprentice glassblowers. Here Paul, with the help of his family, began experimenting with paperweight making.

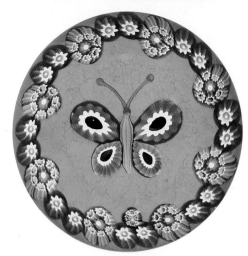

Millefiori butterfly with a cane garland

In 1948, Salvador and his sons Vincent and Augustine started their own business called Ysart Brothers Glass in Perth. Paul continued on at Moncrieff, where he created some of the finest paperweights made since the nineteenth century. In 1963 he took a job with Caithness Glass in northern Scotland, continuing to make paperweights in his spare time.

In 1971 Ysart started the Paul Ysart Glass Company in Wick, which specialized in paperweights and other glass objects produced in limited editions. He retired in 1979.

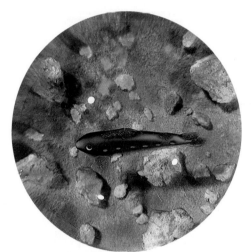

Iridescent fish among pebbles

Over his fifty years of paperweight making, Ysart has produced a wide range of millefiori designs set on clear, colored and lace grounds. One of his favorite motifs is a hovering butterfly. Other subjects include clematis-type flowers, snakes, dragonflies, ducks and swimming fish.

Most of Paul Ysart's weights contain a small "PY" signature cane either in the design or on the base of the piece.

Lampwork flower with radiating latticinio

Major Paperweight Collections Open to the Public

The Art Institute of Chicago
Michigan Avenue at Adams Street
Chicago, Illinois 60603
312 443-3600
Arthur Rubloff's collection of over 1200
paperweights is on permanent exhibit.

Bergstrom-Mahler Museum
165 North Park Avenue
Neenah, Wisconsin 54956
414 729-4658
More than 700 paperweights collected
by Evangeline Bergstrom.

The Corning Museum of Glass
One Museum Way
Corning, New York 14830
607 937-5371
Approximately 500 paperweights from the
collection of Amory Houghton, as well as
an impressive sulphide collection.

Flint Institute of Arts
The DeWaters Art Center
1120 East Kearsley Street
Flint, Michigan 48503
313 234-1692

Glyn Vivian Art Gallery
Swansea, Wales
Approximately 65 weights, mostly antiques,
well displayed.

Historical Society of Old Newbury
Cushing House
98 High Street
Newburyport, Massachusetts 01950
508 462-2681
Part of the Bushee collection; many good
American and French examples.

Illinois State Museum
Spring and Edwards Streets
Springfield, Illinois 62706
217 782-7386
The Morton D. Barker collection of more than
240 paperweights.

New-York Historical Society
170 Central Park West
New York, New York 10024
212 873-3400
Approximately 550 paperweights made up
primarily of pieces collected by Jennie H.
Sinclair.

Saint Mary of the Barrens Seminary
Estelle Doheny Museum
Perryville, Missouri 63775
314 547-6300

Sandwich Glass Museum
P.O. Box 103
Sandwich, Massachusetts 02563
617 888-0251

Seneca County Museum
28 Clay Street
Tiffin, Ohio 44883
419 447-5955

Victoria and Albert Museum
Brompton Road
Kensington
London, England

Wheaton Museum of American Glass
and Wheaton Village
Millville, New Jersey 08332
609 825-6800

Glossary

Air ring An elongated air inclusion encircling a weight near the base, usually above and below a torsade.

Annealing oven An oven that gradually reduces the temperature of the finished piece to ensure even cooling and prevent cracking.

Arrow cane (or **Crow's-foot**) A millefiori section made from rods containing a three-pronged arrow motif.

Aventurine Glass with a sparkling appearance caused by the addition of metallic crystals to the melt.

Basal rim The ring around the bottom of a concave base where the paperweight comes into contact with the supporting surface.

Basal ring The flange seen on some English paperweights, a result of in-cutting just above the base, not a footed weight.

Base The bottom of a paperweight.

Basket An outer row of millefiori canes, pulled together underneath the motif to form a staved enclosure for the decorative elements; a latticinio ground pulled down in the center (as in Saint Louis and American fruit weights); a latticinio ground with a "handle" of twisted filigree extending above the motif.

Batch A mixture of sand, lead oxide, potash, and cullet within the melting pot.

Block (or **Paddle**) A curved wooden paddle used to shape the dome of a paperweight.

Blowtorch (or **Lamp** or **Torch**) A small gas burner or torch used to reheat hardened crystal rods for lampwork motifs.

Bouquet A floral design composed of more than one flower.

Bouquet de mariage A mushroom motif in which the tuft of the mushroom is composed of white stardust canes.

Cabbage rose A Clichy rose composed of cabbagelike strands of glass that may have been formed in a rose-cane mold.

Cameo See **Sulphide**

Cameo incrustation Any type of sulphide object.

Candy Denotes a scrambled millefiori paperweight.

Cane (or **Floret**) A small piece of molded or bundled glass rod that has been pulled out and cut so that an intricate pattern appears in cross section.

Carpet ground An overall pattern of identical millefiori canes used as a ground.

Chaplet bead A twist of latticinio thread.

Chequer weight A paperweight in which the millefiori canes are separated by short lengths of latticinio twists in a checkerboard fashion.

Choufleur From the French for cauliflower; a kind of ground made up of canes set loosely and with a twist. See also **Ground.**

Chrysoprase Apple green in color.

Cinquefoil A garland of canes having five loops.

Circlets Small circles of millefiori canes.

Classic period Paperweight production in France between 1845 and 1860.

Clear ground Clear glass used as a background for a paperweight design.

Close concentric A spacing pattern in millefiori weights with tightly packed concentric circles of canes.

Close packed (or **Close millefiori**) A tightly packed arrangement of millefiori canes.

Clover cut Intersecting facets, typical of the surface cutting of the New England Glass Company.

Cluster A close grouping of similar canes, common in certain Clichy paperweights.

Cog cane A molded millefiori cane with a serrated edge.

Cog method A special notation for the identification of Saint Louis paperweights.

Collar A metal ring used to surround the disc or template and to help center the motif being picked up by molten crystal.

Color ground Opaque or transparent colored glass used as a background for a paperweight motif.

Concentric Any spacing scheme in millefiori weights with concentric circles of canes placed around a central cane or cluster of canes.

Cookie base A thick, cookie-shaped pad forming the base of fruit weights made by the New England Glass Company.

Crimp A metal tool inserted into molten glass to form three-dimensional roses and lilies, used especially at Millville.

Crimped cane A corrugated or vertically ribbed cane.

Crown (or **Dome**) The glass above the motif in a paperweight.

Crown weight A type of hollow paperweight in which alternating bands of colored and lacy white twists radiate from a central floret near the top of the dome, flow down the sides of the weight, and converge again near the base.

Crow's-foot See **Arrow cane**

Crystallo-ceramie The patented name and process for cameo production developed by Apsley Pellatt. See also **Sulphide.**

Cullet Small pieces of broken glass added to the batch.

Cushion See **Ground**

Cutting Grinding the surface of a paperweight for ornamentation.

Date cane A millefiori cane with numerals or a letter identifying the year of manufacture.

Decorative paperweight A paperweight produced in unlimited editions, usually unsigned or signed with a paper seal, and moderately priced for beginning collectors; not investment quality.

Design The internal decoration of a paperweight.

Devil's fire A swirling, mottled motif used by Millville.

Diameter The most commonly used physical measure of a paperweight.

Diamond cut See **Grid cut**

Disc See **Template**

Dome See **Crown**

Doorstop A very large paperweight, primarily manufactured by English bottlemakers and American glasshouses in the midwest.

Double overlay See **Overlay**

Edelweiss cane A white star-shaped millefiori cane surrounding a core of bundled yellow rods; resembles the Swiss national flower.

Encased overlay See **Overlay**

End-of-day See **Scrambled**

Facet (or **Printy** or **Punty**) The flat or concave surface formed when the side or top of a paperweight is shaped with a grinding wheel. Printy usually refers to a concave facet.

Faceting Flat cutting of the domed surface of a paperweight.

Festoon A swag design used especially in marbrie weights.

Filigree See **Lace**

Flash A thin coating of transparent colored glass applied to the base of a paperweight; applied to the entire weight in the case of a flash overlay.

Flat bouquet See **Nosegay**

Floret See **Cane**

Flower weight A paperweight in which a single flower is the central motif.

Fluting A pattern of deep, narrow grooves usually cut vertically on the outside of a paperweight.

Footed weight (or **Pedestal weight** or **Piedouche**) A weight having its own pedestal, flanged on the bottom.

Furnace A tank fabricated for melting the glass batch.

Gaffer A skilled craftsman; a master glassworker.

Garland Any spacing scheme using one or more chains of millefiori canes in an undulating pattern.

Gather Molten glass collected on the end of a pontil rod.

Gauze See **Lace**

Glory hole A fabricated unit with an intensely hot flame used for reheating glass.

Gold inclusion A gold or enameled gold design enclosed within crystal.

Goldstone A gold aventurine glass used primarily by Italian glassmakers.

Grid cut (or **Diamond cut** or **Strawberry cut**) A series of shallow narrow grooves cut into the base of a paperweight to form a grid.

Ground (or **Cushion**) A cushion on which the decorative element of a paperweight rests; usually convex in appearance when viewed through the top or sides of the weight.

Handcooler A solid or hollow blown egg-shaped glass object; once a common accessory for women.

Hobnail A series of V-shaped grooves cut into the base of a paperweight at right angles to each other, forming a grid pattern.

Hollow weight A blown weight with a central hollow air bubble surrounded by glass. Used in crown weights and to encase lampwork figures.

Honeycomb cane A type of millefiori rod, the cross-section of which resembles the cell pattern of a honeycomb.

Incrustation The process of enclosing a sulphide in glass.

Initial cane See **Signature cane**

Intaglio A decoration either pressed or cut into a piece of glass.

Jasper ground Ground formed by a mixture of two colors of finely ground glass.

Lace (also called **Filigree, Gauze, Muslin, Upset muslin**) White or colored glass threads spiraled around a clear rod; used in short segments to form a paperweight ground.

Lamp See **Blowtorch**

Lampwork The manipulation of glass with a gas burner or torch; also the process of creating representational paperweight subjects.

Latticinio A lacy backdrop created from white and clear glass. Lace is uniformly chaotic, whereas latticinio is a basketweave pattern.

Lattimo Opaque, white milk glass.

Macédoine A paperweight containing primarily filigree twists.

Magnum A paperweight with a diameter exceeding 3¼ inches.

Marbrie (or **Marbled**) A paperweight design consisting of looped, colored bands emanating from a cane at the top of the weight and running along the sides to the bottom. Design elements are close to the surface of the dome.

Marver A smooth, flat iron surface (formerly made of marble) on which the gather of molten glass at the end of a pontil rod is rolled.

Mazarene blue A purplish blue similar to ultramarine, used as a ground or overlay color.

Melt A batch of molten glass.

Metal Traditional term used by glassworkers for glass in its molten state.

Millefiori Italian word for "a thousand flowers," the cross-sections of molded glass rods of various sizes and colors used in paperweights.

Millefleurs French term for **Millefiori.**

Miniature Paperweight with a diameter of less than two inches.

Molds Precast iron forms of different geometric designs, animal silhouettes, initials, numerals, and other shapes, into which a gather of molten glass is pressed to create a cane design.

Moss cane A complex cane composed of green rods, sometimes centered around a white rod.

Mushroom (or **Tuft**) A paperweight containing an upright mushroom-shaped tuft of millefiori canes.

Muslin See **Lace**

Newel post A paperweight post at the end or foot of a flight of stairs, supporting a handrail.

Nosegay (or **Flat bouquet**) A paperweight motif consisting of a flat bouquet using millefiori canes as flowers.

Opaline A flat rectangular or book-shaped paperweight, made of opaque or transparent opaline glass, with a slightly raised oval medallion, nosegay, or other millefiori design encased within; a specialty of Clichy.

Overlay A paperweight that has been coated with one (**Single overlay**), two (**Double overlay**), or three (**Triple overlay**) layers of colored glass, with windows cut on its coated surface to allow visual access to the inner motif. Encased overlays have been further covered in a thick coating of clear glass.

Paddle See **Block**

Panel weight A paperweight in which clusters of canes form alternating sections separated either by exposed sections of the weight's ground, filigree twists, canes, or rods.

Paperweight A glass sphere or plaque enclosing decorative elements such as millefiori canes, lampwork motifs of colored glass, sulphide portraits, or metallic motifs.

Pastry mold A millefiori cane that flares or "skirts" out at its basal end.

Patterned Any spacing scheme in millefiori weights with ordered groupings of florets forming a design.

Pedestal weight See **Footed weight**

Pell-mell See **Scrambled**

Penholder (or **Shot glass**) A paperweight-based, short flanged vase, originally filled with shot to be used to hold quill pens.

Piedouche French term for **Footed weight.**

Pinchbeck weight A metallic disk made of a zinc-copper alloy simulating gold or silver, with a design in bas-relief. The disc is covered with a magnifying lens fitted to a pewter or alabaster base.

Not a true glass paperweight because the motif is not entirely encased in glass.

Pontil mark (or **Pontil scar**) The characteristic mark in the center of a weight's base, where the weight was separated from the rod on which it was made.

Pontil rod A long, solid metal rod, usually made of iron, used to hold a paperweight while it is being made.

Profile The shape of a paperweight viewed from the side.

Printy See **Facet**

Punty See **Facet**

Quatrefoil A four-lobed design used as the central element of a millefiori cane; a faceting scheme for the exterior ornamentation of some paperweights; a garland pattern.

Random spacing scheme An assortment of canes packed tightly together in an upright position to form an overall design.

Reduction lathe A complex mechanism that cuts a reduced and faithful reproduction of an original bronze image into steel, used in sulphide production.

Reduction lens Used in sulphide production to check the surface smoothness of a cameo.

Refractory pot A fireproof clay receptacle used to melt the components of glass at 1400–1450° C, used for two or three months before being replaced.

Ribbon A cane containing a flat ribbon-like element, sometimes twisted; used in crown weights, torsades, and chequer weights.

Ring A row or circle of millefiori canes in a concentric paperweight.

Rock ground (or **Sand ground**) An uneven granular paperweight ground formed with unfused sand, mica flakes and green glass.

Rod A cylindrical length of glass, most often containing a simple molded design of more than one color; the basic component of a millefiori cane.

Rose pompadour A delicate pink ground used in some Clichy paperweights as well as Sèvres porcelain.

Rosette A central motif of closely fitted canes in a circular cluster, symbolizing a flower.

Saliva Unwanted string of air bubbles from insufficient expulsion of air during assembly.

Sand ground See **Rock ground**

Scattered millefiori A somewhat irregular spaced concentric millefiori pattern.

Scrambled (or **End-of-day** or **Pell-mell**) A millefiori paperweight design in which whole and broken canes and sometimes white or colored lace are jumbled together to fill the weight.

Servitor An attendant or helper.

Setup Used interchangeably with "motif" to denote the central element(s) in a representational weight.

Shears A scissors-like instrument used to cut malleable glass.

Shot glass See **Penholder**

Signature cane (or **Initial cane**) A millefiori cane indicating the name or initial(s) of the weight's factory of origin or the artist who created it.

Silhouette cane A millefiori cane that reveals the shape of an animal, flower, or figure when cut in cross section.

Single overlay See **Overlay**

Spaced millefiori A pattern of individual millefiori canes set at equal or nearly equal distances from each other, forming a set of vaguely defined circles.

Spacing schemes Motifs of millefiori canes in random, patterned, and special arrangements.

Spiral An opaque glass thread wound around a clear rod.

Spiral latticinio A convex or funnel-shaped ground formed by threads of latticinio.

Spoke concentric A New England Glass Company design suggesting spokes of a wheel.

Spoke paperweight One with an overall design suggesting the spokes of a wheel; a Saint Louis paperweight having a jasper ground of alternating colors divided by spokelike tubes.

Star cut A many-pointed star incised into the base of a weight for decoration.

Stardust cane A cane composed of tiny star-shaped rods separated by clear glass, usually surrounding a geometric cane center.

Stardust ground A ground made up a white star rods.

Star paperweight A weight with an overall star-shaped design, a Clichy specialty.

Stave A flattened glass tube, used to form basket motifs and Clichy roses.

Strawberry cut See **Grid cut**

Striae (or **Striations**) Streaks of glass of different optical quality caught in the dome of a paperweight, giving the glass an undesirable sugary or grainy appearance.

Sulphide (or **Cameo**) A three-dimensional ceramic medallion or portrait plaque used as a decorative enclosure in paperweights or other glass objects.

Swirl weight A paperweight design with opaque colored rods of two or three colors radiating in pinwheel fashion from a central millefiori floret, giving it a flat appearance.

Table facet A flat circular cut on the top of a weight.

Tank See **Furnace**

Tazza (or **Wafer dish**) A dish supported by a stem or foot, the bowl or base of which is made of millefiori canes, used to hold wax seals.

Template (or **Disc**) In paperweight production, a small cast iron disc on which the motif is carefully arranged before being picked up.

Thumbprint cut An oval, elongated concave window.

Torch See **Blowtorch**

Torsade (or **Twist**) An opaque glass thread loosely wound around a filigree core, usually found near the base of a mushroom weight.

Trefoil A garland with three loops.

Tricolore Originally the red, white and blue French flag of 1789; later, paperweights with flowers in these three colors, popular during the Revolution of 1848.

Triple overlay See **Overlay**

Tuft See **Mushroom**

Twist See **Torsade**

Upright bouquet Three-dimensional grouping of canes and stylized lampwork flowers set on a bed of leaves.

Upset muslin See **Lace**

Venetian ball A Venetian scrambled paperweight made of millefiori leftovers that have been rolled into a ball and covered with glass.

Wafer dish See **Tazza**

Waffle cut A series of wide perpendicular cuts made in the base of a paperweight.

Whorl rod A millefiori cane component with a spiral cross-section; often used as the center of a cluster of star rods.

Window A facet on an overlay paperweight.

Select Bibliography

Annual Bulletins of the Paperweight Collectors' Association. New York: Paperweight Collectors' Association, 1955–.

Baccarat, Inc. *A History of Baccarat Modern Paperweights.* New York: Baccarat, 1977.

Bedford, John. *Paperweights.* New York: Walker and Company, 1968.

Bergstrom, Evangeline H. *Old Glass Paperweights.* Chicago: The Lakeside Press, 1940; Crown Publishers, 1947.

Catalogues of paperweight sales at Christie's, London; Sotheby's, London and New York; L. H. Selman Ltd., Santa Cruz, California.

Cloak, Evelyn Campbell. *Glass Paperweights of the Bergstrom Art Center.* New York: Bonanza Books, 1976.

Elville, E. M. *Paperweights and Other Glass Curiosities.* 2nd ed. London: Spring Books, 1967.

Glass Paperweights of the Bergstrom-Mahler Museum. Richmond, Virginia: United States Historical Society Press, 1989.

Hollister, Paul, Jr. *The Encyclopedia of Glass Paperweights.* New York: Clarkson N. Potter, Bramhall House, 1969.

―――. *Glass Paperweights of the New-York Historical Society.* New York: Clarkson N. Potter, 1974.

Hollister, Paul, Jr., and Dwight P. Lanmon. *Paperweights: "Flowers which clothe the meadows."* New York: The Corning Museum of Glass, 1978.

Imbert, Roger, and Yolande Amic. *Les Presse-Papiers Français de Cristal.* Paris: Art et Industrie, 1948.

Ingold, Gérard. *The Art of the Paperweight—Saint Louis.* Santa Cruz, California: Paperweight Press, 1981.

Jokelson, Paul. *Antique French Paperweights.* Privately published, 1955.

―――. *One Hundred of the Most Important Paperweights.* Privately published, 1966.

―――. *Sulphides: The Art of Cameo Incrustation.* New York: Thomas A. Nelson, 1968.

Jokelson, Paul, and Gérard Ingold. *Paperweights of the 19th and 20th Centuries.* Phoenix, Arizona: Papier Presse, 1989.

Jokelson, Paul, and Dena K. Tarshis. *Cameo Incrustation: The Great Sulphide Show.* Santa Cruz, California: Paperweight Press, 1988.

―――. *Baccarat: Paperweights and Related Glass 1820-1860.* Santa Cruz, California: Paperweight Press, 1990.

Kovacek, Michael. *Paperweights.* Vienna: Glasgalerie Kovacek, 1987.

Kulles, George N. *Identifying Antique Paperweights—Lampwork.* Santa Cruz, California: Paperweight Press, 1987.

———. *Identifying Antique Paperweights—Millefiori.* Santa Cruz, California: Paperweight Press, 1985.

Mackay, James. *Glass Paperweights.* New York: Viking Press, 1973.

Manheim, Frank J. *A Garland of Weights.* New York: Farrar, Straus and Giroux, 1967.

Mannoni, Edith. *Classic French Paperweights.* Santa Cruz, California: Paperweight Press, 1984.

McCawley, Patricia K. *Antique Glass Paperweights from France.* London: Spink and Son, 1968.

———. *Glass Paperweights.* London: Charles Letts & Co., 1975.

Melvin, Jean Sutherland. *American Glass Paperweights and Their Makers.* Rev. ed. New York: Thomas Nelson, 1970.

Paperweight News. Santa Cruz, California: Paperweight Press, 1975–.

Pellatt, Apsley. *Curiosities of Glass Making.* London: David Bogue, 1849. Reprint: Newport, England: The Ceramic Book Company, 1968.

Penwell, Ellen Schaller. *The Morton D. Barker Paperweight Collection.* Springfield, Illinois: Illinois State Museum, 1985.

Revi, Albert Christian. *Nineteenth Century Glass.* New York: Thomas Nelson & Sons, 1959; rev. ed., 1967.

Rossi, Sara. *A Collector's Guide to Paperweights.* Secaucus, New Jersey: Wellfleet Press, 1990.

Selman, Lawrence H. *The Art of the Paperweight—Perthshire.* Santa Cruz, California: Paperweight Press, 1983.

———. *Collectors' Paperweights—Price Guide and Catalogue.* Santa Cruz, California: Paperweight Press, 1975, 1979, 1981, 1983, 1986.

———. *The Art of the Paperweight.* Santa Cruz, California: Paperweight Press, 1988.

Selman, Lawrence H., and Linda Pope-Selman. *Paperweights for Collectors.* Santa Cruz, California: Paperweight Press, 1975.

Smith, Francis Edgar. *American Glass Paperweights.* Wollaston, Massachusetts: The Antique Press, 1939.

Turner, Ian, Alison J. Clarke and Frank Andrews. *Ysart Glass.* London: Volo Edition, 1990.